T0286765

Cambridge Elements ☰

Elements in Greek and Roman Mythology
edited by
Roger D. Woodard
University of Buffalo

DISABILITY AND HEALING IN GREEK AND ROMAN MYTH

Christian Laes
University of Manchester

CAMBRIDGE
UNIVERSITY PRESS

Shaftesbury Road, Cambridge CB2 8EA, United Kingdom

One Liberty Plaza, 20th Floor, New York, NY 10006, USA

477 Williamstown Road, Port Melbourne, VIC 3207, Australia

314–321, 3rd Floor, Plot 3, Splendor Forum, Jasola District Centre,
New Delhi – 110025, India

103 Penang Road, #05–06/07, Visioncrest Commercial, Singapore 238467

Cambridge University Press is part of Cambridge University Press & Assessment,
a department of the University of Cambridge.

We share the University's mission to contribute to society through the pursuit of
education, learning and research at the highest international levels of excellence.

www.cambridge.org
Information on this title: www.cambridge.org/9781009494663

DOI: 10.1017/9781009335560

First published 2024

A catalogue record for this publication is available from the British Library.

ISBN 978-1-009-49466-3 Hardback
ISBN 978-1-009-33553-9 Paperback
ISSN 2753-6440 (online)
ISSN 2753-6432 (print)

Cambridge University Press & Assessment has no responsibility for the persistence
or accuracy of URLs for external or third-party internet websites referred to in this
publication and does not guarantee that any content on such websites is, or will
remain, accurate or appropriate.

Disability and Healing in Greek and Roman Myth

Elements in Greek and Roman Mythology

DOI: 10.1017/9781009335560
First published online: April 2024

Christian Laes
University of Manchester

Author for correspondence: Christian Laes, christian.laes@manchester.ac.uk

Abstract: *Disability and Healing in Greek and Roman Myth* takes its readers to stories, in versions known and often unknown. Disabilities and diseases are dealt with from head to toe: from mental disorders, to impairments of vision, hearing, and speaking, to mobility problems and wider issues that pertain to the whole body. This Element places the stories in context with due attention to close reading and to concepts and terminology regarding disability. It sets Graeco-Roman mythology in the wider context of the ancient world, including Christianity. One of the focuses is the people behind the stories and their 'lived' religion. It also encourages its readers to 'live' their ancient mythology.

Keywords: Greek and Roman mythology, ancient history, disability history, ancient medicine, history of religion

ISBNs: 9781009494663 (HB), 9781009335539 (PB), 9781009335560 (OC)
ISSNs: 2753-6440 (online), 2753-6432 (print)

Contents

Introduction

Greek and Roman mythology almost spontaneously elicits the image of powerful gods, mighty heroes, and frightful creatures whose stories have been told time and again in epic descriptions and exciting tales that seem to fascinate enduringly a large audience with very different backgrounds and interests. In popular books, interest in classical mythology has been revived by what has been called 'the paraphrase industry'. Such works often leave unmentioned how value-loaded the term 'classical' by itself is, since it presupposes a kind of superiority of Greece and Rome over, say, the Egyptian, Indian, or Mesopotamian mythological traditions. Much more than to tantalising stories about divine superpower and heroic endeavours, this Element will turn its attention to human beings and the way they cope with the interaction/tension between religion on one hand and matters of health perceived as irregularities/defects on the other. It will do so by placing the Greek and Roman mythological stories within the larger frame of comparative religious science, not the least the Judaic and Christian traditions.

For such a quest, clarity of concepts and terminology is of key importance. In Section 1, I thus ask about crucial notions of disability, mythology, and religion. I also deal with the question of whether people in antiquity actually 'believed' their myths. Broadly speaking, the potential contradiction between divine or heroic status and physical defects runs through the Indo-European tradition of myth and belief. In Section 2, I take a practical approach, narrating the stories of disabled gods and heroes by applying a scheme 'from head to toe' with due attention to so-called combined disabilities. In Section 3, I focus on 'less traditional' disabilities such as twins, people of different stature, or the sorrows of old age. It is often claimed that the fear of 'pollution' would require bodily integrity and wholesomeness of those performing cultic acts. In Section 4, I scrutinise this assertion. In Section 5, I look at the role of monotheism, particularly of Christianity in late antiquity, in order to see how far the Christian approach towards disability and religion differed from pagan views and practices. Since healing also assumed an important role in the new religion, the intermingling of divine power and bodily suffering was possibly perceived differently.

1 Setting the Scene: Disabilities, Myths, and Religion

1.1 The Problem of Disabilities

Sooner or later – preferably sooner – any student of disabilities in the premodern world faces the problem of defining the term. For this, one can turn to a definition such as that developed by the World Health Organization.[1] It immediately becomes clear, though, that such organisations handle very broad criteria that are hardly applicable to the ancient world, including, for instance, social disabilities and learning disorders. However, when the student of disabilities turns their attention to ancient concepts and terminology, they will find there is hardly any equivalent Greek or Latin word for the umbrella term 'disability' of the present-day era. To put it more boldly: it seems as if ancient peoples did not know disabilities (which of course does not mean that they did not acknowledge the difficulties of experiencing bad vision or impaired mobility). The concept of disability before, say, the nineteenth century is indeed an anachronism. Only from this period on had states in the Western world viewed the nation as a healthy body, for which they required sound citizens. At the same time, those who did not fulfil the desired ideal were categorised as *dis-abled* or *dys-functional* – the medical label often provided them with care and support by the same nation state.

Such labels did not apply to antiquity. Rather than studying what is termed a disability, some ancient historians therefore prefer to study difference in the ancient world – leading them to careful considerations of bodily conditions that were viewed as undesirable, as opposed to the concept of bodily integrity. Studies of difference cover a very wide field, as many categories fit this bill: being a woman, a child, or a 'barbarian foreigner'; being branded as a criminal; or exercising a profession or skill that lacked dignity in the eyes of Greek or Roman elite writers. Such a study of difference is not the task of the present Element. While fully acknowledging the intricate difficulties in using the term 'disability', I rather continue the path set out by anthropologists and ethnologists, who usually distinguish the following categories:

1. Mobility impairment
2. Sensory impairment (visual and auditory)
3. Speech disorders
4. Learning disorders and/or intellectual impairment
5. Mental disabilities
6. Multiple impairments (often a combination of the categories just mentioned).

Of course I do not want to ignore the objections of using these categories for a study of the past.

The first objection is epistemological. In line with Paul Veyne (1930–2022), scholars of ancient religions and mentalities have claimed that historians can never really access the *Ding an Sich*. It is thus quite unhelpful to state that

---
[1] www.who.int/health-topics/disability#tab=tab_1.

people in the past also experienced, say, blindness or difficulties with walking. What is left to study is the interaction of people with 'the facts'. According to Veyne, 'matters of fact' are always intrinsically linked to interpretation. There is no way an historian can ever disentangle the knot between the two. In line with anthropology, I prefer to observe the distinction between the etic and the emic – an approach that in my view takes primarily into account the corporeality of human existence, and at the same time argues against naïve positivism. It acknowledges, for instance, that in all cultures and times, some people faced difficulties with vision (etic), but at the same time realises that reactions and responses to this varied significantly across different cultures (emic). In the same way, ancient historians have successfully studied phenomena such as (homo)sexuality or racism, while terminology and concepts regarding these are very much related to biological approaches of the nineteenth century too.

The second objection is more ethically inspired, driven by justified concerns about accessibility, inclusion, and human rights. Following Michel Foucault (1926–84), scholars have claimed that the mere mention of the word 'disability' always involves an instinctive judgement about who is considered able and who is not. Choices for terminology are inevitably ideologically loaded, and users are not always aware of this. Such differentiation especially turns up in deprecatory vocabulary, with terms such as 'cripple', 'retarded', 'simpleton', or 'imbecile'. These words have now vanished from the public discourse. Others are increasingly branded as politically incorrect: 'handicap' is considered inappropriate, and we might envisage the same happening eventually to 'disability' too. This moral attention to language and vocabulary has the great merit of making us aware of our prejudices and the way we almost unconsciously judge other people, who might feel offended and hurt by our careless use of terms. Yet there also lurks a danger in this moral approach. Too often, the mere naming of a disability, even the use of the term itself, is reproached as a form of ableism. The reproach of ableism fits into a typically Western and Christian anthropology of blaming oneself and emphasising one's own culpability. Recently, it has been claimed that the Greeks should be held responsible for the promotion of perfect bodies as an aesthetic ideal and the concomitant aversion to those who did not meet the ideal – an unjustified claim in my view. As I will explain in the Conclusion, we risk a scenario in which only Western culture is prepared to undermine a category such as health or ability that almost all other cultures take for granted (the same counts, mutatis mutandis, for male/female or old age). In other words, I do not necessarily regard it degrading to notice that someone lacks certain abilities because they are not able to see, hear, or walk. Banishing words such as 'blind' or 'deaf' is not helpful in promoting the inclusion and functioning of such people in human society – a concept of integration I fully endorse. It also is not beneficial to rephrase systematically terms such as 'visually challenged' or 'rebellious/challenged' bodies, particularly in a study about the past. Behind this might even be a tendency towards denial of suffering, an essential part of the human condition. One cannot simply state that it does not really matter whether one sees or is not able to see – very few would prefer the latter condition. This said, my frequent use in this Element of terms such as 'blind', 'deaf', or 'speech disorder' is in no way judgemental, but I hope to do justice to a condition of human life that was observed and recognised in the case of people from the past, as evidenced by their myths and stories.

1.2 On Gods and Myths, and Whether People Believed in Them

By now, entire libraries are filled with books about religion in the Greek and Roman worlds. This multiform and polytheistic belief was profoundly different from how most readers of this Element, coloured by their European and Christian background, presumably understand religion. In more than one way, a contemporary Hindu believer from India would experience less difficulty in understanding ancient beliefs. Ancient religion was mostly anthropomorphic. It was religion without dogma. There was no fixed set of beliefs. There were no 'official' interpretations one had to stick to, nor overarching institutions such as a church with its full hierarchy. The concept of conversion was virtually absent. A strict distinction between the sacred and the profane was never made: the gods and divine power were working within the world. No strict barrier existed between religion and ordinary life. Religion made few ethical demands: little notion of sin, no prescribed rules of life, no denial of worldly pleasures. All this is not to say that sin and repayment for transgressive behaviour did not play a role in myths about disability and suffering. In his first book of *Histories*, Herodotus (*c*.485–425 BCE) famously narrates the story of the decline and fall of the Lydian king Croesus, who had a deaf-mute son whose name is never mentioned. Croesus paid for the sins committed four generations earlier (*Hist.* 1.13). Oedipus' father, Laeus, was said to have brought a curse on his house and descendants by abducting and raping Pelops' son Chrysippus, thus abusing the hospitality and guest-friendship Pelops had offered (Apollod. *Bibl.* 3.5.5).[2] In fact, stories featured in works such as Daniel Ogden's *The Crooked Kings of Ancient Greece*

---

[2] I have referenced the relevant articles for the disabled gods and heroes dealt with. In the text, I refer to specific primary sources whenever they are used. For the readers who wish to track down these references, I have duly used the abbreviation system of the Oxford Classical Dictionary (fourth edition, 2012). All translations are from the Loeb Classical Library (for the Bible, I used the Douay–Rheims translation). I always mention the name of the translator. When no name is given, the translation is my own.

(1997) abound with examples of divine punishment (and disability) for transgressive deeds and behaviour.

Myths were the foundational stories of religion. They were popular tales in which gods, demigods, and heroes, as well as monstrous creatures, all figured. In antiquity, myths were employed as ideological tools, much as they are today. In our search for 'standard versions', we often think of myths as a static category. Standard versions of them, however, have never existed. In selecting some parts of a story and suppressing others, communities revealed a lot of their shared values and preferences. In this process, cultural identity was often at stake. Also, we should refrain from the desire to distinguish sharply between gods, heroes, and historical figures. In the ancient collective phantasy, most myths were at least partly 'historical'. The line between individuals and divine aspirations could be thin. For instance, the Hellenistic cult of the rulers partly had its base in the deification of Alexander the Great, while Ovid's *Metamorphoses* ends with the divine transformation of Julius Caesar. As Helen Morales aptly put it: 'What makes someone mythic is not whether or not he lived, or lived well, but whether he was larger than life. Mythic heroes were . . . outrageous and outstanding. They are phenomenal' (2007: 55). Mythological heroes thus embodied the phantasies of the people. They mattered, not only for the past, but also for the present.

Myths have been studied (and criticised) from antiquity on, and in the past centuries, they have been scrutinised in psychoanalytic, structuralist, metaphorical, allegorical, institutional, and ritual approaches, to name only a few. For the Greek part, the fascinating stories masterfully narrated by Homer (presumably eighth century BCE) and Hesiod (between 750 and 650) had such power as to become almost canonical, though their versions were never imposed and many divergent and local traditions continued to exist next to them. The same can be said for the selected versions of mythological plots adapted by the Athenian tragedy writers Aeschylus (*c*.525–456), Sophocles (496–406), and Euripides (*c*.480–406). Their plays were hugely successful and continue to be influential up to the present time. Due to this success, the story about Medea killing her children after she was betrayed by her husband, Jason, resonates in contemporary culture, while this was actually Euripides' invention. In other versions, the mother Medea protects her children.

A treasury of mythological traditions was later compiled by mythographers such as Apollodorus (second century BCE?) and Antoninus Liberalis (second–third century CE) in Greek and Hyginus in Latin (first century BCE–first century CE?). Their striving after the mythological correctness of standardised versions was a misguided undertaking. Mythological stories were always creatively told and retold, and there simply is no way to standardise or even give priority to one particular version.

For the Roman side, Virgil's (70–19) *Aeneid* or Ovid's (43 BCE–17 CE) fascinating collection of stories ending with Caesar's transformation, the *Metamorphoses*, next to his unfinished calendar, the *Fasti*, can be regarded as the most influential literary works that gave shape to the mythological tradition. Long passed are the days in which scholars claimed that the Romans, sober and level-headed peasants by origin, had never known any real native mythology but only took it over from the Greeks at a later stage. Since a diaspora brought Greeks to the Italian peninsula as early as the eighth century BCE, it would be a mistake to search for any 'autochthonous' or 'primitive' Roman religion. Intermingling with foreign elements took place from the early beginnings. In addition, it makes little sense to restrict mythology to stories about gods in order to claim that the Romans had none. Romulus killing his twin brother, Remus, King Numa Pompilius having the nymph Egeria as a divine partner, and the battle between the Roman Horatii brothers and the Curiatii from Alba Longa – they were as much part of Roman collective memory and belief as was the Trojan War for the Greeks. To the ancients, these events had truly taken place. As such, the first book of Livy's (59 BCE–17 CE) monumental history *From the Founding of the City* was as much mythology as were Homer's *Iliad* or *Odyssey*. As for the tradition about the first Roman king, Romulus, adapting from the Greeks a much 'purer' concept and practice or religion, this is to be ascribed to the 'pious' admiration of the Greek writer Dionysius of Halicarnassus (*c.*60 BCE–after 9 CE) for the superpower that Rome had become in his days under the reign of Augustus. I will come back to Dionysius' fundamental text in Section 5.

Did the ancients believe in their gods? Did they believe in the myths? This is a complex question, yet at the same time essential to the subject of this Element. It is made even more complex because of the fact that we draw much of our information about religion from the literary sources, products of a highly atypical elite who lived a life of leisure and pleasure with far more comfort than the huge majority of the population. The attention to other written sources such as papyri and inscriptions only slightly remedies this shortcoming, and it remains difficult to make firm statements about 'lived religion' with the middling or the poorer classes in the Greek and Roman worlds. Here, the study of depictions of mythological scenes on all sorts of artefacts, not the least on relatively less expensive vases, may offer some remedy.

The frivolous story about Hephaestus, god of the blacksmiths, who caught red-handed his beautiful but adulterous wife, Aphrodite, the goddess of love, while she was having sex with Ares, the god of war, will be dished up in Section 2.5 (Hom. *Od.* 8.266–366). Would Homer's or a later ancient audience have believed that the event really happened? In addition, would they accept the existence of cheating and jealous gods, with a limping blacksmith cunningly taking revenge for the offence of adultery?

It seems undeniable that most Greeks and Romans believed that there were indeed powerful gods, who very much existed, as do human beings. Though neither supremely good nor just, these gods had to be worshipped, in part because it could be dangerous not to do so. Thousands of votive inscriptions or objects testify to bargains between humans and their gods. Recent scholarship has strongly focused on these particularly revealing instances of 'lived' religion. In return for a benefit, such as a healing, people would compensate the god they had invoked, or simply turn to another deity if the favour was not immediately granted. Throughout the ages, the denial of a godly blessing has led people to despair and (temporarily) disbelief. 'Say, do you really believe in the gods?', says a house slave to his fellow (Ar. *Eq.* 32). 'To you who reads this and who doubts whether gods of the underworld exist. Take a vow and call us. Then you will understand', we read on a funerary inscription set up in Rome by a freedman who lost his children at early ages. We are told that the dedication was made after a dream vision (*ex viso*; *CIL* 6.27365).

Social historians of nineteenth- and twentieth-century French parish life have repeatedly pointed out the existence of outsiders who stubbornly refused ever to attend Mass. Obviously, their religious context was fundamentally different from the Greek and Roman period, but the same pattern of not believing might have been behind it. In all, it is very difficult to assess the personal beliefs of an individual of the past, and it is virtually impossible to do so for those not belonging to the upper classes that are so overrepresented in the ancient sources.

As regards the elites from the sixth century BCE on, we see tendencies towards a more sophisticated reading of the myths, shying away from literal interpretations and anthropomorphism. An itinerant poet himself, the Greek philosopher Xenophanes (*c.*570–*c.*478) reproached Homer and Hesiod for having ascribed to the gods everything that is shameful and disgraceful about human beings: stealing, committing adultery, and cheating (fr. 11). He observes how Aethiopians picture their gods as snub-nosed and black, while Thracians imagine them to be blue-eyed and auburn-haired (fr. 16). In his purified image of the divine, a god is a creature that sees, hears, and knows everything – an apparent criticism of polytheism too (fr. 24).

Stories about the battles of giants, centaurs, or Titans belong to the realm of tales of the older generations (fr. 1). As far as we can tell from the fragments that survive, Xenophanes' criticism of anthropomorphism never mentioned the case of disabled gods, though later on, (Neo)Platonic and Stoic philosophers would try to come to terms with the representation of the lame god of fire, Hephaestus. Other famous critics of traditional religious concepts include Heraclitus (*c*.540–*c*.480) (who in fr. 128 states that the statues of *daimones* cannot hear), and the Athenian cases of Anaxagoras (*c*.500–*c*.428) and Socrates (470/69–399). In the case of the two last named, we know of trials for the impiety of not believing in the gods. In the depiction of his ideal state, Plato (*c*.427–347) pleaded for the banishing of stories in which gods or heroes set a bad example or behave badly (*Resp.* 377a–8a).

In the Hellenistic period, Euhemerus (?–*c*.280 BCE) advanced his theory of god and man in a fictional travel book entitled *Sacred Scripture*. He claimed that Uranus, Cronus, and Zeus had once been great kings and that they were later on worshipped as gods by the grateful people (Diod. Sic. 6). A similar theory about the invention of religion by Sisyphus as a spin doctor in order to keep the bad people quiet and obedient already appears in an Athenian play of the fifth century BCE, which we know only in fragmentary state (Critias, fr. 25).

The same story of scepticism, criticism, and allegorical interpretations of myth can be told about Roman leading figures: Caesar (100–44), Cicero (106–43; with outstanding treatises on religions such as *On the Nature of the Gods* or *Concerning Divination*), or writers such as Plutarch (46–119 CE). They were not seldom inspired by allegorical interpretations of myths in the Stoic tradition, or admonitions against unfounded fear for the gods with the Epicureans. The tradition continues with Christian writers like Origen (*c*.185–253/4) or Augustine (354–430), who obviously take the opportunity of mocking pagan anthropomorphism in order to promote the validity of Christian faith.

Yet we should be very cautious about interpreting these critiques of myths and religion from an Enlightenment perspective, let alone an atheist one. In fact, the opposition between *muthos* and *logos* and the transition 'from-myth-to-logic approach' is an invention of eighteenth-century scholarship and of later presumptions about 'unsophisticated' peoples moving on to a more developed stage of thinking. Despite his moralising criticism of myth, Plato would continue to use myths in his philosophical discourse, and some of the myths of his own invention resonate up to the present (for example, the Allegory of the Cave, the myth of Er in his *Republic*, or the myth of the original androgyne in the *Symposium*). To Aristotle, there is a fundamental similarity between the 'wondering questions' addressed by myths and by philosophers (*Met.* 2.982b11–19). The critics of the ancient writers rather are concerned with the nonsensicality of anthropological tarnishing and divisive polytheism. They call for a purified understanding of the divine.

In any given society, there often is not one agreed-upon truth. Rather, many certainties exist at the same time, all of them containing some truth. Contrasting and even contradicting stances and viewpoints exist within every single human being (some contemporary medical doctors rely on homeopathic medicine too; some scientists accept miracles and the Resurrection in their personal Christian belief, horoscopes and fortune telling remain popular) – intellectuals are no exception to this, as they were not in the ancient world. As a learned physician and philosopher, Galen (129–*c*.216) could simply not believe in centaurs, as no one had ever seen them (*De optima secta ad Thrasybulum* 3; 1.110 K.). According to him, believing in such creatures would be absurd. Yet when he describes the origins of medical science in Greece, the same Galen mentions without hesitation the god Apollo, teaching the art to his son Aesculapius, and the centaur Chiron, who had educated the Greek heroes about some remedies belonging to the noble art of medicine (*Isagoge seu medicus* 1; 14.675 K.).

Ancient literature indeed abounds with references to what a modern reader would anachronistically label as superstitious: the credulous parvenu Trimalchio claims to have seen the Cumaean Sibyl hanging in a bottle (Petr. *Sat.* 48), while the aristocrat Pliny the Younger (61–*c*.113) extensively treats ghost tales in one of his letters (Plin. *Ep.* 7.27). Despite their attention to inconsistencies in myths and creeds (the geographer and traveller Pausanias (*c*.115 CE–180 CE) investigated the veracity of the stories about giants, as to whether they were divine creatures or human beings; 8.29), ancient writers hardly ever went so far as to utterly deny the myths. Indeed, few authors would have believed that Odysseus actually blinded the Cyclops, that Theseus fought the Minotaur, or that Numa Pompilius regularly spoke to a nymph. But they would most probably agree with Plutarch's comparison: truth/myth equals sun/rainbow (*De Iside* 358f).

The history of atheism in antiquity is not the subject of this Element – and in fact is a difficult one on which to write. The poet Diagoras of Melos (fifth century BCE), who was known as an *atheos*, actually did not deny the existence of the divine, but was sceptic about many representations of it. The gods were meant to be worshipped in one way or another and the myths retained a certain value. This is what happened indeed. Irrespective of tendencies towards henotheism and divine power without mythology that turn up in late antiquity from the late second century on, Greek and Roman myths continued to resonate despite the victory of Christianity in the later period of the Roman Empire. In fact, they do so up to now.

1.3 Wounded and Disabled Gods: A Widespread Tradition

Wounded and disabled gods make irregular appearances in Greek and Roman mythology. They even stand at the very beginning of the Greek tradition. In the first chapter of his *Mythological Library*, Apollodorus summarises the story of

Hesiod's *Theogony*. The union between Uranus (Heaven) and Gaea (Earth) produced three awesome creatures, the Hecantonchires, each of whom had 100 hands and 50 heads. After them were born three Cyclopes, each with one eye on his forehead. After the Cyclopes' banishment to the underworld, Uranus had another six sons and seven daughters with Gaea: the Titans. As a mother, Gaea had never forgotten the exile of her sons, the Cyclopes. In a conspiracy of the Titans, the youngest son, Cronus, emasculated his father, Uranus, by cutting off his genitals with a sickle and throwing them into the sea. We do not hear of any healing of Uranus, who continued his immortal life, unmanned and unthroned.

Combat, wounding, and elimination are also at the heart of the second battle for succession, with again the youngest son, Zeus, resisting his father, Cronus, who had swallowed all his other children in fear they would expel him from the throne. With the help of the Cyclopes and the Hecantonchires, Zeus, together with his brothers and sisters, eventually won over Cronus and the Titans. Locked up in the underworld, Cronus would carry on as a rather symbolic god of time and eternity. In the aftermath of the struggle, Gaea tried to regain power by bringing in the frightful giants. No gods themselves, they were not only wounded in battle, but also eliminated (Apollod. *Bibl.* 1.6).

As far as immortality is concerned, there appears to be a strict dividing line between gods and other creatures. No god could ever attempt suicide, while a survey of heroes and heroines of Greek mythology numbers, respectively, fifty-one attempts (thirty-seven completed) and seventy-one (fifty-six completed). Yet immortality could not protect them from incurable wounds and everlasting punishment, such as the Titan god Prometheus who, in chains, had to endure the consuming of his liver by an eagle during daytime. Since the organ was restored during night-time, the torture was perpetual until Heracles made an end to it (Figure 1).

Wounded gods frequently appear in the *Iliad* too. Aphrodite is hurt by Diomedes while she protects her son Aeneas (Figure 2). The Greek hero realises that Aphrodite actually is not the kind of deity that is superior in war against human beings (Hom. *Iliad* 5.329–38). *Ichor*, the blood of the immortals, flows out of her wrists (5.340). In anger and pain, Aphrodite rides to Olympus to seek comfort with her mother, Dione, only to find out that other gods too have been hurt by mortals (5.359–404). Ares had been confined to a copper vessel for thirteen months by the sons of the giant Aloeus and was at risk of dying (5.388). Hera was most painfully hurt by an arrow with three barbs shot in her chest by Heracles, as was Hades by a fierce arrow deep in his shoulder shot by the same fearsome Heracles – we are informed that despite his pains, immortal Hades could simply not die (5.402). In the same vein, hot-tempered Diomedes threw his spear at Ares. Guided by Pallas Athena, the weapon gravely wounded Ares in the stomach. The god screamed with the voices of 10,000 men and sought

Figure 1 Prometheus bound. Black-figure Lakonian kylix, *c.*570–560 BCE, depicting the Titans Atlas carrying the world on his shoulders and Prometheus being tormented by an eagle sent by Zeus to eat his liver as punishment for giving mankind the gift of fire, stolen from Hephaistos (Gregoriano Etrusco Museum, Vatican). www.worldhistory.org/image/1149/prometheus-atlas

Figure 2 Aphrodite protecting Aeneas. Attic red-figure calyx, *c.*490–480 BCE. Diomedes battles Aeneas, who is wounded in the thigh. The goddess Athena – equipped with spear, helm and aegis cloak – supports the hero. Aphrodite rushes forward with arms outstretched to rescue her son, but will be wounded in the arm by Diomedes (Museum of Fine Arts, Boston). www.theoi.com/Olympios/AphroditeMyths2.html

refuge at Olympus (5.855–68). In the presence of Zeus, Ares bewailed Athena's act – even holding forth the possibility that he might be permanently impaired because of his war wound.

'But my swift feet carried me away; otherwise I would surely have long suffered woes there among the gruesome heaps of the dead, or else had lived strengthless (*amenēnos*) through the blows of the spear' (Hom. *Iliad* 5.886–7; transl. A. T. Murray).

Zeus's reply to Ares' laments was hardly what one would call sympathetic, but since Ares was his son, he could not allow him to suffer so deeply. He thus ordered Paeëon to heal him with his herbs. Ares was swiftly healed, and afterwards bathed and clad in beautiful clothes by Hebe and could again sit down by the side of Zeus in full glory (5.887–906). We are also told that Ares could not have died anyway, since he was not of mortal flesh (5.901). That such was not always an asset is pointedly formulated by Ovid: 'It is a dreadful thing to be a god, for the door of death is shut to me, and my grief must go on without end' (Met. 1.662–3: transl. F. J. Miller – Inachus, the father of Io, is speaking).

Absence of suffering, disease, or disability is part of the early Greek tradition too. Those of the golden race, in the times of the god Cronus, spent their lives as gods. They never grew old and always enjoyed the same strength in their hands and feet. Dying was just like falling asleep (Hes. *Op.* 109–26). The silver race was not like their predecessors. They enjoyed a childhood of 100 years, but in adulthood lived only for a short period, in pain because of their folly, which consisted in respecting neither themselves nor the immortal gods (127–42). Terrible and strong were the members of the bronze race, but their lust for war and bronze armour soon drove them to Hades (143–55). The race of demigods was the generation before Hesiod's. They also were destroyed by battles and death, though on some Zeus bestowed happy and eternal life on the Island of the Blessed at the limits of the earth (156–73). As for Hesiod's own generation, the iron race: 'If only then I did not have to live among the fifth men, but could have either died first or been born afterward!' (Hes. *Op.* 174–5; transl. G. W. Most).

Toil and distress by day and suffering at night are part and parcel of their condition. The race will eventually end when at birth the hair on their temples will be grey. By then, respect and reverence towards their fathers will have gone, and Zeus will destroy this generation too.

In Section 2, some wounded and disabled Greek and Roman gods or heroes will be highlighted. As a last point for this introductory section, it is important to note that such gods and stories are in no way unique to the Graeco-Roman tradition. It is enough to consult older monumental and wide-ranging comparative studies of mythology and religion such as the *Golden Bough* by Sir James

George Frazer (1854–1941) or *The Mythology of All Races*, edited by Louis Herbert Gray (1875–1955).

Disabled gods indeed make for fascinating stories. In Norse mythology, Hodur, son of Odin and Frigg, was congenitally blind, which caused him to stand outside the circle of men although he was of sufficient strength (Figure 3). He is tricked by Loki to shoot an arrow of mistletoe towards his brother Baldr. In fact, the mistletoe was the only existing thing that had abstained from swearing never to slay the seemingly invulnerable Baldr. The arrow struck Baldr. For this unintentional killing, Hodur was sent to Hel. The case of Baldr may even be an exception to the rule that gods do not die (if they do, they rise again, as Frazer claimed of the Egyptian Osiris, the Greek Adonis, and Dionysus or Attis in the Phrygian tradition). The *Prose Edda* alludes to Hodur's death or slaying in Hel's realm – thereby foreshadowing the doom of the gods (Ragnarök). Of all creatures, only the old giantess Thokk refused to mourn for him.

In the tradition of comparative Indo-European studies, no scholar has worked more on the theme of disabled gods than George Dumézil (1898–1986). His attention was particularly drawn to gods or heroes who had lost their right hand ('the One-Handed') or an eye ('the One-Eyed'). Examples of the former will be

Figure 3 Blind Hodur. Loki tricks Hodur into shooting Baldr. https://en.wiki pedia.org/wiki/H%C3%B6%C3%B0r

included in Section 2. Traditions about the latter category, the One-Eyed, abound too. As a symbol of bravery in battle, the Irish warrior Cûchulainn closed one of his eyes so that it was almost invisible, while he made the other incredibly big. One eye of the Norse Odin was sunk in the fountain of Mimir, which gave him wisdom, knowledge of runes and magic. The Roman Horatius Cocles, defender of the bridge at the Ianiculus, had one eye and was therefore compared to the Cyclopes (Dion. Hal. *Ant. Rom.* 2.18). The Hindu god Bhaga lost both eyes at a primordial sacrifice, though they were restored later on. Recompensation is key to understand Dumézil's interpretation of such myths: most of these gods give up or sacrifice a part of their body for a higher cause, and they are rewarded for it with a higher fame and sometimes with items that replace the amputated or lost part of the body.

2 Disabled Gods and Heroes 'from Head to Toe'

The order of appearance of gods and heroes figuring in this section is 'from head to toe'. Following the ethnographical pattern sketched out in Section 1, I start with mental disabilities and then proceed with afflictions of the eyes, the ears, and the mouth, and end with mobility impairment. For each deity or hero, I ask the same questions. First is the cause of the impairment. Was it congenital, or rather the consequence of an accident, incident, or deliberate bravery? Second is whether the affliction was narrated and depicted as a disability, or rather as a characteristic of the god which did not really matter or hinder. Next is whether the deity in question was worshipped with emphasis on their disability, or whether this was again rather viewed as an incidental characteristic. Finally, cure and restoration or possible compensation are highlighted. In discussing these tantalising stories, I am fully aware of the dazzling variety of versions that circulated in a world where no standardised, let alone dogmatic, reading ever existed. For finding out about this variety, scholars of antiquity are fortunate enough to be able to rely on rich encyclopaedias and handbooks, some going back to the nineteenth century, which brought together an incredible treasury of data that we can now approach with 'new' questions in mind.

2.1 Madness with Gods and Heroes

Starting off with the head and mental disabilities, we immediately face enormous methodological issues. Classifications tend to differentiate between mental and intellectual impairment, but a sharp distinction is difficult to make even in contemporary medicine, let alone for the ancient world with the limited sources we have at our disposal. 'Madness' is a notoriously vague term which can simply be used jocularly or to humiliate one's opponent without any symptoms that would fit a modern medical diagnosis. Also, the work by E. R. Dodds has convincingly showed how the irrational – or at least what we consider it to be – was part and parcel of the ancient world. For alteration of consciousness, ancient Greeks sometimes used the term 'divine *mania*', a concept which implied that it was sent by the gods. There were many terms for this particular mental state, and they were all discussed extensively by the writers, not the least philosophers: prophetic *mania*, embodied religious experience related to the mystery cults, collective ecstatic *mania* as in the Bacchic rites, fury on the battlefield, *mania* related to the nymphs and Pan, erotic *mania*, and the manic passion of philosophers on their way to the truth.

Greek mythology is full of tales about temporary madness and sudden rage. Tragic madness comes as a divine punishment, as a temporary and episodic rage. Delusion, violent activity, intermittent loss of consciousness and physical features as wild eyes, shaking, or frothing of the mouth were symptoms of it. Heracles was struck by temporary insanity and consequently killed his wife and children: 'He was no longer the same person. His face was distorted, his eyes rolled in their sockets, their veins filled with blood, and drool began to soak his bearded chin' (Eur. *HF* 931–4; transl. R. Garland).

In verse 822, we are told that the goddess Lyssa was bringing on the rage. Ajax was struck by distorted vision by the goddess Pallas Athena (Soph. *Aj.* 51–2 mentions 'evil fancies'). She induced him to slaughter cattle, believing that he was fighting Agamemnon and Odysseus. Shame and embarrassment about the deed lead him to suicide. What disturbed him most were the laughter and the humiliation he would provoke (*Aj.* 367). In Bacchic ecstasy, Agave and the maenads mistake Pentheus for a wild beast. Possessed by Dionysus, they tear him limb from limb (in Eur. *Bacch.* 851 and 977, Lyssa and her dogs again figure). In his gruesome lust for murder and revenge, Orestes proceeded with killing his mother Clytemnaestra (Aesch. *PV* 881 mentions Lyssa). Both Sophocles and Euripides – the former in his *Ajax* (207–333), the latter in the *Heracles Furens* (1140–1227) and *Bacchae* (1263–99) – in gruesome and painful detail describe how the perpetrators, once insanity had disappeared, came to realise what they had done. More prosaic is the description of the writer and traveller Pausanias of a sanctuary of the Maniae on the way from Megalopolis to Messene. It was the place where madness allegedly overtook Orestes after the matricide. Close to the sanctuary was the Tomb of the Finger, where Orestes in rage and anger bit off one of his fingers. Adjoining this place was another sanctuary for the Eumenides, who were called the Acê ('Remedies'). Here, Orestes was cured of his insanity. First, when they wanted to drive Orestes insane, the goddesses had appeared to him in black shape. After he had bitten off his finger, they appeared to him as white figures, and so he recovered his senses (Paus. 8.34).

All these stories mention gods as the agents of the madness induced. Apart from well-known deities such as Dionysus and Pallas Athena, we also encounter Lyssa and Mania (who is often considered as one of the Furies, also known as the Erinyes who were euphemistically called Eumenides 'Gracious Ones'), to whom could be added other personifications such as Oistros ('Rage') in Greek and Furor ('Fury') in Latin (Figure 4). Yet it should be stressed that they never were 'mad deities' themselves. In depictions on vases, we see them as young women, sometimes huntresses, accompanied by dogs, or as demonic characters with a frightful gaze. In the literary sources, they often appear with poets, as personifications of anger, rage, and madness. They are hardly ever worshipped on inscriptions. As such, the tradition of 'mad gods' was non-existent in the Graeco-Roman world, while 'divine madness' per se was fully recognised in many instances, also in the case of worshipping gods. There seem to be remarkable similarities with other religious traditions of the ancient world. In the Hindu tradition, 'madness' was the mark of at least some of the devotees of Krishna. Such does not make Krishna a mad god himself. The same counts for the Egyptian tradition. Here,

Figure 4 Lyssa. Attic red-figure krater, *c.*440 BCE. Lyssa, goddess of madness, from a painting depicting the death of the hunter Actaeon. Lyssa is depicted as a Thracian huntress a short dress, high boots, an animal-skin vest and fox-head cap (Museum of Fine Arts, Boston). www.theoi.com/Daimon/Lyssa.html

depictions of the dwarf god Bes, more especially the deity's protracted tongue, have sometimes been interpreted as a token of intellectual disability. This seems like too bold an assumption, though: over a period of 2,000 years, there is not one single mythological story about Bes. Scholars have interpreted the iconography and imagery of him in multiple ways, allowing for many more possibilities than 'a mad god'.

A special case of mental disability and healing is the possible occurrence of post-traumatic stress disorder (PTSD) in Greek tragedies. In Euripides' *Ion*, the Athenian princess Creusa recalls being raped by Apollo. While she is in Athens, it feels as if she is reviving that atrocious experience in a cave at Delphi – a painful flashback, as many victims of PTSD describe (247–51). When her son, Ion, asks what is bothering her, she prefers not to speak about it and asks him not to worry too much (256–7), again a well-known reaction. Even more: later on, she mentions a friend of hers who claimed to have gone to bed with Apollo (338). The substitution of the self, by narrating the story as if it had happened to someone else, is a well-known strategy of coping too. Only at the end of the play does Creusa realise that she just cannot continue to cover Apollo's hideous deed in silence, though she is afraid of the embarrassment that will go with the disclosure of it (859–61). She now literally relives the sexual violence and in the course of her narrative switches to the present tense (885–901). Scholars of Greek tragedy have pointed to the possibility of both Euripides and his audience recognising the psychological suffering of women after rape in the war-struck city of Athens of the year 413 BCE, when the play was staged. A similar awareness of PTSD, now from the side of the war veteran, may have been at stake in Sophocles' *Ajax*, probably performed in 442 or 441 BCE, and mentioned earlier (Figure 5). The scene of the hero facing the slaughtered cattle, unwilling to eat or drink and considering harming himself (323–6), looks very similar to the experiences of those who committed killings in war and are later on confronted with the results. Ever since the Vietnam War, therapists and theatre productions have returned to staging Greek tragedies in order to offer help to those experiencing PTSD by either restaging the play with victims as actors or reading in small groups or even in individual therapy. Such experiments, with reportedly good success, are remarkable instances of the perpetual strength and valour of Greek imaginary, mythology, and tragedy. As Aristotle already noticed (*Poet.* 1449b), 'pity' (*eleos*) and 'fear' (*phobos*) arise when watching or reading such plays, whence later on comes *katharsis*: a reconciliation of strong emotions on one side and rational reflection about them on the other. Instead of a mere slogan, *Achilles in Vietnam* thus became a powerful tool for coping with contemporary issues of healing.

Figure 5 The Suicide of Ajax: Etrurian red-figure calyx-krater, *c.*400–350 BCE, presumably from Vulci (British Museum, London). https://en.wikipedia.org/wiki/Ajax_the_Great#/media/File:Ajax_suicide_BM_F480.jpg

2.2 Blind Gods

It does not take an aficionado of world mythologies to know that godly creatures with visual impairment occur in some cultures. In Section 1, we encountered comparative evidence of one-eyed heroes and gods in the Irish, Norse, and Roman traditions. I also mentioned the Norse Hodur, who in his blindness was tricked to shoot a lethal arrow in the direction of his brother Baldr. For Egypt, the story of Horus, who lost one eye, the so-called *udjat* eye, in the fight with his rival, Set, is quite well known.

When one seeks a Graeco-Roman equivalent of blind deities, it turns out that they are hard to find. In fact, the only feasible counterpart would be Plutus, the god of wealth. However, even for this deity, the evidence on visual impairment is meagre, to say the least. In Hesiod's *Theogony*, Plutus is the son of Demeter and the hero Iasion. As a kind god, he brings wealth to the people who cross his path (Hes. *Theog.* 969–74). In the Homeric hymn to Demeter, we are told that the bright goddess from Olympus, where she dwells with Zeus and the other gods, sends Plutus to give wealth to blessed men who are loved by the gods (*Hymn Hom.* 6.488–9). There is no mention of blindness in these early testimonies. Yet in a deprecatory fragment, the sixth-century BCE poet Hipponax complains about Plutus, who is depicted as 'exceedingly blind' and with 'a coward's mind' too (the Greek could also mean 'dim-witted'), who never bothered to visit the poet's house, granting him wealth in the form of thirty minas of silver (fr. 36). Already with Hipponax the blindness of Plutus seems to have become a commonplace. But one immediately sees the problems that such personification involves. Is the poet really thinking about a god? Or are we faced with a cliché – both ancient and modern – as if saying that Love or Fortune are blind (notice the capitalisation of both names, though manuscripts of ancient writers obviously are not clear about whether we should read a particular noun as a proper name with a capital letter). A somewhat similar deprecation of Plutus, calling him blind and responsible for all evils that inevitably accompany him, turns up in a drinking poem against Wealth by Timocreon of Rhodes in the fifth century BCE (fr. 731). The standard depiction, however, of Plutus as a blind god, stems from Aristophanes' comedy named after the god, performed for the first time in 408 BCE and again on stage in 388 BCE. The plot is rather straight-forward. On his return from the oracle of Delphi, the Athenian Chremylus encounters Plutus, who turns out to be a blind old man. He persuades him to attend a sanctuary in Piraeus, where he eventually gets healed. The play is full of intended reversals and metaphors. Right from the beginning, Chremylus is following Plutus, while one would expect that it is the blind man who needs a guide (Ar. *Plut.* 13–16). Plutus is not only old, but also filthy, toothless, stooped (thus also mobility impaired), and pitiable (*Plut.* 265–6) – 'stinking rich' is an expression that survives up to today, while the image of the lonely old man without family as heirs may have played a role too. To make matters worse, Aristophanes even suggests that the god of wealth might be circumcised, as were barbarians (*Plut.* 267). We are informed that it was Zeus who brought this 'evil' to him. When Plutus was a boy, he had vowed that he would 'only visit the houses of just, wise, and decent people'. Now Zeus made him blind in order to keep him from recognising any of them. In his conversation with Chremylus, Plutus solemnly pledges that, if he were to see again, he would definitely turn away from the wicked and only visit the just (*Plut.* 86–98). Plutus is then healed at the Asclepius sanctuary in the Piraeus (*Plut.* 727–34). Yet what happens when Wealth sees again? All want to pay him honours: the just man who got ruined (*Plut.* 828–49), but also the wicked informer who is short of money (*Plut.* 850–76). The Athenian audience would have understood the message: basically, all people are blinded by wealth. 'They say that Wealth is blind, since we see that the rich are out of their mind,' says a scholion to the Greek poet Theocritus (*Scholion* 10.19a, p. 230 Wendel). Aristophanes' metaphor is a powerful one, and his play was successful. The power of his images vibrates up to today, but it may have obscured the role of Wealth in Greek religion. In fact, we do not have a single ancient depiction that portraits Plutus as aged. Neither is there any trace of blindness, although the Christian author Clement of Alexandria reports that painters represented him as blind (*Protr.* 10). In iconography, Plutus mostly appears as a boy with a cornucopia, who sometimes is handed over by a female figure to another god, often Hermes (Figure 6). As the son of Demeter, he appears in the Eleusinian mysteries, with a little temple in his honour north-east from the Telesterion. Only two altars with Greek inscriptions for Plutus survive: one from Pisidia, and one from Lydia, respectively from the Roman and the Hellenistic period. Here Wealth is mentioned in connection with other gods, as he nearly always is in the literary records and on coins too.

Aristophanean themes and motives play at the background of Lucian's *Timon or the Misanthrope*, a satirical dialogue of the second century CE. The Athenian Timon laments his own poverty. He once was rich but has distributed all his wealth to friends. Zeus and Hermes hear his prayers, and they bring in Plutus. Yet Wealth replies that Timon had 'made ducks and drakes of me'. All the money went into the hands of parasites and prostitutes (Lucian. *Timon* 12). Here one notices the very thin line between allegory, popular-philosophical personification, and worship: Plutus actually *is* the money spent. Later on in the dialogue, we learn that Wealth is not only blind, but also lame. Again allegory comes in. Plutus is indeed slow and sluggish when he has to visit someone. But

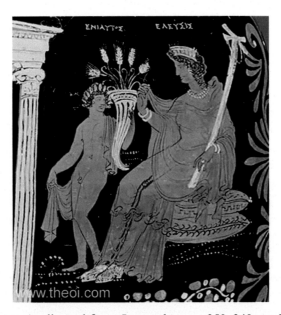

Figure 6 Plutus. Apulian red-figure Loutrophoros, *c.*350–340 BCE. The goddess Demeter, seated and holding a four-headed Eleusinian torch, is labelled 'ELEUSIS', as queen of the Eleusinian Mysteries. Her son Plutus, here named 'ENIATOS' (Year), holds a cornucopia (horn of plenty) bursting with heads of grain (The J. Paul Getty Museum, Malibu). www.theoi.com/ Georgikos/Ploutos.html

when Wealth leaves he has wings (*Timon* 20). When Hermes asks Plutus how he, as a blind person, manages to find the way to the persons to whom Zeus sends him, the obvious reply is that he actually just wanders up and down. Thus Plutus admits to cheating Zeus (*Timon* 24). Hermes now asks how a blind, pale, and heavy-footed man can have so many admirers and lovers. The answer again is predictable. Ignorance and deceit cause people to be 'blinded' by wealth and not actually see its real appearance (*Timon* 26–7). The 'disabling' effects of blindness (and mobility issues) are not what prevails in Lucian's dialogue. To the ancient readers, the symbolic aspect of Plutus' physical appearance stood at the foreground.

Yet with this rather specific case of personified Wealth, the catalogue of blind Graeco-Roman gods already comes to an end. True, the giant Cyclopes, children to Uranus and Gaea, were one-eyed or rather orb-eyed (Hes. *Theog.* 143), but this is never mentioned as a disabling feature. As for the younger breed of Cyclopes, the blinding by Odysseus of the principal Cyclops Polyphemus, who had one eye on the forehead, is staged in Euripides' satyr play *Cyclops*. To the amusement of the audience, the victim gropes his way around the stage, following the useless indications of the choir. He is mocked and ridiculed and bangs his head on a rock (Eur. *Cycl.* 682–7). Throughout Greek and Roman history, individuals known to have had only one eye were called Cyclopes: Philip II of Macedon (382–336), Antigonus I (382–301), the philosopher Timon of Phlius (*c.*320–230), Dionysius the Elder (*c.*432–367), the tyrant of Syracuse who was rather known for his poor eyesight, and Roman emperors such as Maximinus Thrax (r. 235–8) and Firmus (r. 372–5). In an interesting attempt at empathy dispersed with humour, the Hellenistic poet Theocritus (*c.*300–after 260) narrates Polyphemus' courtship of the beautiful nymph Galatea. Polyphemus realises she is running away from him because of his long single eyebrow stretching from one ear to the other and his one eye. Later on, he understands that his looks are not as bad as people say. He describes how he used the sea as a mirror and was not really displeased by what he saw (*Id.* 6.30–8). In a similar representation of the myth, Ovid describes Polyphemus being careful about his physical appearance and not disliking himself when seeing his own reflection in a pool – all this the Cyclops himself brings forward in an attempt to convince and conquer Galatea by words (*Met.* 13.764–869). With Lucian, we even read about Galatea defending her relationship with the Cyclops, whom she actually finds manly, with his eye befitting the forehead (*Dial. D.* 1). We have here a remarkable instance of a mythological creature who became emblematic: both to nickname certain individuals who, presumably, were not always pleased with the denomination, and as a symbol of ugliness which could be overturned by stressing the positivity of other physical features.

2.3 Blind Individuals in Legends and Myths

Was there any blind god in Roman mythology? As mentioned, Horatius Cocles, who fought for the Roman Republic by defending the bridge against the Etruscans and the former royal family of the Tarquinii, in one tradition was said to have had only one eye (cf. supra p. 14). The story is possibly a remnant of Roman mythology of a far distant past which Roman historiographers had converted into the history of early Rome. The same can be said for Caeculus, the mythical founder of the city of Praeneste. His mother was impregnated by a spark of fire from the hearth next to which she was sitting. Exposed as an infant, he was found, lying next to a fire, by a group of girls, who handed the little boy over to his uncles, twins, in order to be reared. Since the boy was found unharmed by the fire he was considered a son of Vulcanus, the Latin version of Hephaestus. Due to the smoke to which he was exposed, his eyes would always remain small – hence the name Caeculus, 'a little blind' (Servius Honoratus, *In Aeneidem* 7.678). Along with the element of twins, the rest of his life story echoes the Roman foundation myth: spending his youth among shepherds, he would gather a band of young men and found a new city, Praeneste. As a master of Latin and Christian rhetoric, Tertullian (*c.*160–after 220) rages against pagan beliefs and practices he finds absurd. What to think of a certain Caeculus who takes away the light of the eyes of people, presumably at the moment of death (*Ad nat.* 2.15)? We can hardly know if Tertullian made this up to defame pagan worship – we have no other traces of a god named Caeculus in our sources, and this passage establishes no link whatsoever with the founder of the city of Praeneste.

For blind individuals in myth, the Greek tradition certainly has more to offer. Blinding as a divine punishment indeed has a long tradition in Greek myth. The perpetrators sometimes were men. Thus Orion was blinded by Oenopion, since he had raped his daughter (or wife in another version). His sight was restored by Helios. Phoenix, the later educator of Achilles, in his youth had sex with his father's concubine. Blinded by his father, the centaur Chiron restored Phoenix's sight. Melanippe had twins with Poseidon, which outraged her father. Her consequent blinding was reversed by the god of the sea himself. Women resort to this extreme measure too. A startling account of war trauma, despair, and utter grief, both with Euripides and Ovid, is the story of Hecuba, former queen of the fallen city of Troy. When she finds out that Polymestor, king of the Thracians, had killed her youngest son, Polydorus, who was sent to him for safekeeping during the war, she convinces the evildoer and his sons to enter a tent, after which she kills the boys and with her own hand scratches out Polymestor's eyes. In a gruesome scene of Euripides' *Hecuba*, we see the blinded king on stage, stumbling and chasing the queen in vain, like a savage (1066–7 and 1173). Even better known is the self-blinding of Oedipus, using the golden pins he took from Jocasta's dress, when he finds out that he is unintentionally guilty of parricide and incest (Soph. *OT* 1268–85) (Figure 7). There are little or no indications in either Sophocles' *Oedipus Tyrannus* or *Oedipus Coloneus* that through his blindness Oedipus was granted insight into his error (which was not even a personal failure in the sense of the Aristotelean *hamartia*, since he was not and could not be aware of his misdeeds). On the contrary, pity for Oedipus' miserable condition prevails, also on the part of the Athenians, with whom he sought refuge (Soph. *OC* 255–6 and 555–9). The disabling effect of his blindness is strongly emphasised too in Euripides' *Phoenissae* (1530–9) and in Seneca's *Oedipus Rex*, where it is compared to the death penalty (936–51), note that verse 1019 explicitly states that fate is to blame and that no individual can be held accountable for Oedipus' bad fortune). Ancient literature thus offers very few indications for a symbolic reading of Oedipus' blindness. The examples quoted make clear how blindness was

Figure 7 Blind Oedipus. Bénigne Gagneraux, *The Blind Oedipus Commending His Children to the Gods* (1784) (Nationalmuseum, Stockholm). https://en.wikipedia.org/wiki/Oedipus_Rex#/media/File:B%C3% A9nigne_Gagneraux,_The_Blind_Oedipus_Commending_his_Children_ to_the_Gods.jpg

Figure 8 Blind Homer. The figure of Homer, as depicted on Raphael's
Parnassus (1509–11) (Vatican Museums, Vatican). https://en.wikipedia
.org/wiki/Homer#/media/File:Cropped_image_of_Homer_from_
Raphael's_Parnassus.jpg

considered the worst of evils. The compensation of it might be the restoring of
the sight: by divine intervention (as with Orion or Melanippe) – or maybe the
gift of soothsaying.

Graeco-Roman mythology indeed preserves accounts of blind poets and
seers (Figure 8) The former includes the blind bard and singer Demodocus
(Hom. *Od*. 8.63–82), who stood as a model for Homer himself, who according
to certain traditions was blind (*Hymn Hom*. 3.172). For the latter, the Theban
seer Teiresias no doubt is the most famous instance. Traditions on his blindness
vary. The mythographer Apollodorus has beautifully brought together three
versions in an account which is worth quoting in full.

> Now there was among the Thebans a soothsayer, Tiresias, son of Everes and
> a nymph Chariclo, of the family of Udaeus, the Spartan, and he had lost the
> sight of his eyes. Different stories are told about his blindness and his power
> of soothsaying. For some say that he was blinded by the gods because he
> revealed their secrets to men. But Pherecydes says that he was blinded by
> Athena; for Chariclo was dear to Athena (. . .) and Tiresias saw the goddess
> stark naked, and she covered his eyes with her hands, and so rendered him
> sightless. And when Chariclo asked her to restore his sight, she could not do
> so, but by cleansing his ears she caused him to understand every note of birds;
> and she gave him a staff of cornel-wood, wherewith he walked like those who
> see. But Hesiod says that he beheld snakes copulating on Cyllene, and that
> having wounded them he was turned from a man into a woman, but that on

observing the same snakes copulating again, he became a man. Hence, when Hera and Zeus disputed whether the pleasures of love are felt more by women or by men, they referred to him for a decision. He said that if the pleasures of love be reckoned at ten, men enjoy one and women nine. Wherefore Hera blinded him, but Zeus bestowed on him the art of soothsaying (...) He also lived to a great age. (Apollod. *Bibl.* 3.6.7; transl. J. G. Frazer)

This is an intriguing account for more than one reason. In one version, Teiresias' blindness was a divine punishment for his revealing godly secrets. Blindness as a consequence of seeing the sacred is a well-known motif in mythology too, as in Roman traditions about Ilus and Antylus, blinded after having seen the Palladium (Plut. *Parall. Graec. et Rom.* 309f–310a). In Teiresias' punishment by Athena, soothsaying by augury comes as a compensation together with a wooden staff and excellent hearing. Ancient authors indeed wondered how a blind man could interpret the signs of the birds, though certainly he could hear the sounds of the animals. According to Sophocles, it is Teiresias' daughter Manto or a servant boy who helps the seer with visual signs (Soph. *Ant.* 1014: 'as I learned from this boy; for he guides me, as I guide others'; transl. H. Lloyd-Jones), while Aeschylus was aware that interpreting the signs of the fire of sacrifice could obviously not have been one of Teiresias' competences (Aesch. *Sept.* 25). The use of a staff for walking is mentioned on several occasions in tragedies too (the 'cornel-wood' [adj. κράνειος, from κράνον] may be of significance, since in the Roman religion 'cornel' [*cornus*] qualifies as a tree of good omen, an *arbor felix*, Macrob. *Sat.* 3.20.1). With snakes and changing sex, mentioned in the second and third versions, we enter the field of chthonic oracle deities, competing oracles, and male or female priests/soothsayers. The remarkable story had huge potential for humorous interpretation, hence the anecdote about the dispute between Zeus and Hera (note that other mythographers such as Antoninus Liberalis completely leave out the element of blindness and mention Teiresias in a catalogue of those who went through a transformation of gender). Be this as it may, also in this version, blindness comes as a punishment with soothsaying as a compensation. Possibly, living to old age was a compensation too. Already in Euripides' *Bacchae*, Teiresias is an old man in Thebes. He plays a prominent role in the fight between King Laeus and Oedipus – three generations later. And again as a blind seer, he goes on to play an important role in the rest of the Theban saga: in the battle between Eteocles and Polynices, sons of Oedipus; during the resistance of Antigone against her uncle Creon; and even in the second Theban war of the Epigoni – all leading us to the fourth generation. In all the surviving tragedies in which he figures – Sophocles' *Oedipus Tyrannus* and *Antigone*, Euripides' *Bacchae* and *Phoenissae* – Teiresias appears as a wise, respected, and trustworthy figure because of his old age and his formidable knowledge of soothsaying (he was the one, for instance, who knew about Oedipus' patricide and marrying his own mother). His blindness, however, does not appear to have been the reason for such deep respect. In his denial of the horrible truth about his past that is gradually revealed, Oedipus rages against the seer with an unforgettable line: 'you are blind in your ears, in your mind, and in your eyes' (Soph. *OT* 371). We are still far away from connotations of blindness with (divine) insight which will be accentuated in Christian traditions of the blinding of the Apostle Paul, or in radical ascetic traditions of self-blinding as a means to gain deeper knowledge. Indeed, what holds for Teiresias can also be said of poets such as Homer and Demodocus: they were excellent seers/poets *despite of* or *in addition to* their being blind, surely not *because of* their being without vision. The latter interpretation would be a far too optimistic reading of the myths, according to which blindness indeed often was worse than being dead (Soph. *OT* 1368).

2.4 Sensory Impairments: Hearing and Speech

In sharp contrast with blindness, other sensory impairments receive attention only very rarely in Graeco-Roman mythology. Deafness is virtually absent. We hear of a statue in Crete of Zeus without ears, 'for it is not fitting for the Ruler and Lord of all to listen to anyone' (Plut. *De Is. et Os.* 381d; transl. F. C. Babbitt). Harpocrates, as a child version of the Egyptian Horus, is represented on Ptolemaic statuettes and coins from the Hellenistic period (Figure 9). This child deity became increasingly popular in the Roman period, with terracotta figurines spread out over the Roman Empire, even up to India. Both bronze and terracotta figurines

Figure 9 Child Harpocrates. Coin of Emperor Antoninus Pius (138–61), from the year 146–7. Isis on the throne, with Harpocrates on her lap. www.coinarchives.com/a/lotviewer.php?LotID=2209196&AucID= 5317&Lot=253&Val=c8b2611240f749f19b4ebd0c374468b1

and representations on coins depict the god holding one finger before his mouth. In the Egyptian tradition, the gesture refers to eating or speaking. In the first century CE, Plutarch understood it as Isis nursing the child by giving it her finger to suck instead of her breast (*De Is. et Os.* 16). However, Roman authors came to understand it as a gesture of silence (Catull. 74.4; Ov. *Met.* 9.692; August. *De civ. D.* 18.5 – the latter already in a hostile interpretation against paganism). Angerona, an archaic Roman deity whose Angenoralia or Divalia were celebrated on 21 December, was represented on her statue with a sealed bandage over her mouth (Plin. *HN* 3.65). After more than a century, scholars of Roman religion have not agreed on the significance of her bound mouth, hypothesising, for instance, that she was connected to a secret name of Rome which should never be mentioned. Silence of course does not yet make for a deaf god. The almost complete silence on deafness as a disability, also in myths and legends, seems a feature throughout world cultures, as has recently been acknowledged for ancient Chinese culture too.

According to Greek legendary tales, Battus, the founder of Cyrene in Libya, established the city despite his speech impairment (or his inability to speak, according to other versions). Some traditions held that *battarizein*, a Greek verb meaning 'to stutter', was derived from the name Battus, while others stated that the hero was named Battus because of his stutter. Roman stories elaborate on Metellus in his role as Pontifex Maximus, who due to his speech impairment experienced great difficulty in pronouncing the sacred formulas (Plin. *NH* 11.174). Be this as it may, the tradition on stammering when faced with the true and almighty God rather derives from the Judaeo-Christian tradition, with Moses as the eminent example of it.

A practical consequence of being voiceless is provided in two beautiful lines by Ovid, touching on young Io who was turned into a cow: 'But instead of words, she did tell the sad story of her changed form with letters which she traced in the dust with her hoof' (*Met.* 1.649–51; transl. F. J. Miller). Roman mythology provides an example of a nymph becoming mute by divine punishment. Lara or Lala (the latter name referring to 'to prattle') was a daughter of Almo. When Jupiter had turned an eye to the beautiful Naiad Juturna, Lara decided to report this to Iuno, despite her father's interdiction. As a punishment, Jupiter took away Lara's speech and handed her over to Mercury, who would bring her to the underworld, the realm of the silent, in order to become a nymph of the marshes. In Ovid's words: 'Take her to deadland', said he, 'that's the place for mutes. A nymph she is, but a nymph of the infernal marsh she'll be' (*Fast.* 608–9; transl. J. G. Frazer). On the way, Mercury raped Lara. She could only plea with a look since her lips failed to speak. So she became the mother of twins, the Lares Compitales, whose shrines are found at crossroads of neighbourhoods and local communities. She became known as the Dea Muta (Mute Goddess) (Ovid. *Fast.* 585–616). The link between silence and the reign of the dead is a red thread in mythological representation of her. As Tacita (Silent Goddess), Lara is also linked to a somewhat sinister ceremony on 21 February, during the feast days for the dead, called the Feralia. An old hag performed rites in favour of Tacita, involving the binding of enchanted threads together with dark lead, the mumbling of seven black beans in her mouth, the roasting of the head of a small fish, sewed up and pierced through with a needle, and the dropping and drinking of wine. All this was done to preserve a household from the pollution of hostile tongues and unfriendly mouths (Ovid. *Fast.* 571–84). Another tradition links Tacita to Rome's second king, Numa Pompilius, thus rendering an extra cachet of old and venerable tradition to her too. Indeed, in his bringing of gentleness and justice to the new-founded city, Numa was said not only to have regularly consulted Egeria, when introducing rites and divine institutions. According to Plutarch, Numa taught the Romans to pay especial honours to Tacita, whom he mentions as a Muse. He explicitly calls her 'the silent, or speechless one' and refers to the Pythagorean precepts of silence (Plut. *Num.* 8). Tacita's fame runs well into the early fourth century CE. The Christian writer Lactantius made fun of her worship: 'Who could prevent himself from laughing when he hears about a Dea Muta? They say it is her from whom the Lares were born, and they call her Lara or Larunda' (Lactant. *Div. inst.* 1.20.35). The connotation of muteness was clearly still there, though it is hard to know whether Lactantius was mocking pagan creeds in a tradition of cultured men versed in literature, or rather referring to actual worship in his day. The fact that that the Dea Muta was only seldom worshipped on altars or inscriptions should make us cautious about overstating her importance as a deity of lived religion (see, however, Tac. *Ann.* 12.24 for a possible shrine on the Forum Romanum, and some mentions of *Mater Larum* in inscriptions).

2.5 Hephaestus As the Lame or Club-Footed God

The Greek Hephaestus, also known as the Roman Vulcanus, has rightly been called an ambivalent deity (Figure 10). He undoubtedly is the best-known disabled god of the Graeco-Roman pantheon, with depictions of his impairment going back to the earliest literary Greek tradition in the Homeric poems. Wayland the Blacksmith, a somewhat similar character, survives in Old English, Old Norse, and other Germanic literature. Here we hear of a smith who is enslaved by a king but who takes revenge by killing the king's sons and then escapes by flying away in a winged cloak he had crafted himself.

Figure 10 Hephaestus. Attic red figure, skyphos, *c.*430–420 BCE. Detail of Hephaestus riding an ass (Toledo Museum of Art, Toledo). www.theoi.com/ Olympios/Hephaistos.html

In what is the earliest description of disability in Greek literature, Homer tells of how Zeus, during a fight with his wife, Hera, had grasped their son Hephaestus by his foot and thrown him off Mount Olympus (Hom. *Iliad* 1.588–600). After a fall of a whole day, Hephaestus eventually arrived on Lemnos with little life left in him. He was taken care of by the Sintian people and later on made a career as a blacksmith on the island. Ambivalence indeed characterises the passage of the *Iliad* in which the story is dished up. Hephaestus is a trustworthy son and urges his dear mother, while placing a cup in her hand, not to stand up again against Zeus, running the risk of being beaten by her angry husband. After having told the story of his own misfortune, he continues to pour wine to the other gods, from left to right: 'And unquenchable laughter arose among the blessed gods, as they saw Hephaestus puffing through the palace' (Hom. *Iliad* 1.599–600). It is hard not to think of Thersites, whose limb is mocked in the second chant of the *Iliad* (217), or of handsome Ganymedes, who on other occasions used to pour out wine and nectar to the Olympian gods.

Quite a different story is told in *Iliad* 18, where we find Thetis, the mother of Achilles, visiting Hephaestus' palace on Olympus at *Iliad* 18.368–427. She is received by Charis, one of the Graces and the wife of the famed craftsman, and put in a shining chair, elaborated by him. The passage contains telling descriptions. Not only did the god of smiths fashion twenty tripods to stand around the wall of his hall. They had golden wheels beneath the base and functioned automatically: they entered the assembly of the gods at his wish and again return to his house, and were 'a wonder to look on' (373–7; transl. A. T. Murray).

Even more surprising are the 'handmaids made of gold in the semblance of living girls. In them is understanding in their minds, and in them speech and strength, and they know cunning handiwork by gift of the immortal gods. They busily moved to support their lord' (418–21; transl. A. T. Murray).

We are constantly reminded of the hard and strenuous labour of the landlord. When Thetis enters, he rises from the anvil. His body is huge and mighty, but beneath it his tiny legs move nimbly. With a sponge, he wipes away the sweat and the dirt from his face and his hands, and puts on a tunic. Hephaestus tells his wife how he owes the visitor a lot. Indeed it was Thetis who, together with Eurynome, had taken care of the young Hephaestus when he was thrown away by his mother, who tried to conceal her son because of his lameness. Surrounded by the streams of Oceanus, the boy was taught the art of craftmanship for nine years by the two goddesses inside a holy cave. According to Hephaestus, it was now time to pay back Thetis for saving his life. The tradition of *Iliad* 18 is in accordance with the pseudo-Homeric *Hymn to Apollo*, in which Hera reproaches her husband for having given birth to Pallas Athena himself, without her being involved (*Hymn. Hom.* 3.311–30). The child she bore by Zeus, on the contrary, was 'weakly among all the blessed gods and shrivelled of foot, a shame and a disgrace to me in heaven, whom I myself took in my hands and cast out so that he fell in the great sea' (*Hymn. Hom.* 3.317–19; transl. G. Evelyn-White). Again we hear of Thetis and her sisters taking care of the boy – a service they had better not offered, according to the enraged Hera.

Hephaestus appears for the third time in a long story in the *Odyssey*, in a song that the blind minstrel Demodocus sang to indulge the heart of Odysseus and the Phaeacians (Hom. *Od.* 8. 266–366). Hephaestus is married to Aphrodite, who was in a secret love affair with Ares. The couple lay together in Hephaestus' house and thereby shamed the bed of Lord Hephaestus. When Hephaestus was told by Helios about the affair, he went to his smithy and crafted a snare. He spread the bonds about the bedposts. They were fine as spiders' webs so that not even one of the gods would notice them. He departed for Lemnos. Ares returned to the house and slept with Aphrodite. The couple soon realised they were trapped and could not even move their legs. Helios now called back Hephaestus, who immediately summoned the gods so that they could see the spectacle. Poseidon was there, together with Hermes and Apollo. We are told that the female gods had stayed at their homes, ashamed to see the scandal. In his fierce anger, Hephaestus' words are quite remarkable. He shouts out that Aphrodite scorns him because he is lame and instead loves Ares, who is beautiful and strong limbed. 'Yet for this is none other to blame but my two parents – would they had never begotten me' (*Od.* 8.312; transl. A. T. Murray). Again unquench-able laughter arises among the gods as they see the craft of the wise Hephaestus.

In the end, Poseidon manages to persuade Hephaestus to release Ares, who will pay compensation in order to reinstill cosmic order among the gods. Justice was so important that Poseidon was even prepared to pay for it himself if Ares would not. The couple is now released and they leave for, respectively, Thrace and Paphus.

To these Homeric testimonies should be added other traditions regarding the limping god. A truly intriguing assembling of various aetiologies of Hephaestus' lameness appears in the work of mythographer Apollodorus:

> Hera gave birth to Hephaestus without intercourse with the other sex, but according to Homer he was one of her children by Zeus. Him Zeus cast out of heaven, because he came to the rescue of Hera in her bonds. For when Heracles had taken Troy and was at sea, Hera sent a storm after him; so Zeus hung her from Olympus. Hephaestus fell on Lemnos and was lamed of his legs, but Thetis saved him. (Apoll. *Bibl.* 1.3.5; transl. J. G. Frazer)

While we indeed recognise Homeric elements, there are some interesting plots from other traditions (according to Hes. *Theogn.* 927–9, Hephaestus was not even born out of a love union between Hera and Zeus, while in Hyg. *Fab.* 166.1–2, Vulcanus 'denies that he even has a mother').

The detail about Hera being trapped and hung from Olympus turns up in quite different versions. From scattered fragments of lost texts, we can gather how Hephaestus took revenge on his mother who had felt disgust towards him (Hall 2021: 229 has conveniently brought together the different versions of the story). From Lemnos, he sent a fine throne. When Hera sat on it, though, she found herself trapped by a secret mechanism. No other god could free her. Ares went to Lemnos to take Hephaestus by force, but he failed since the blacksmith defended himself with fire. Eventually, Dionysus managed to bring Hephaestus over, after he had made him drunk. He arrived in jolly mood to Olympus, sitting on a donkey. Hera was released by her drunken son, and Dionysus was rewarded the admission to the group of Olympian gods. This is not the only instance in which Hephaestus is associated with comic abuse. There is an interesting literary tradition that calls the iambic metre of the satirical poems by a writer such as Hipponax (sixth century BCE) choliambs – that is, 'limping', 'clubfooted' metre. The poet Hipponax himself was said to have been physically deformed too. Corinthian black-figure vases from the same period have depictions of apparently lame dancers sometimes called *Hephaestoi*. Does this refer to *kōmoi*, ritualistic drunken processions that included deformed entertainers (Figure 11)?

It seems as if Hephaestus is to be pitied: he is mocked and derided in a quite tragic way, works in a dark smithy with the monstrous Cyclopes, and is negatively

Figure 11 Greek *kōmoi*. Komast cup, *c*.575 BCE (Louvre, Paris). https://
en.wikipedia.org/wiki/Komos#/media/File:Komast_cup_Louvre_E742.jpg

connected to ugliness in the physiognomic tradition. On the other hand, there is
empowerment too in the stories about him: the way he managed to be the most
clever of gods by his craftsmanship, or his marriages with Aphrodite, with Charis,
or in yet another tradition with Aglaea, who was one of the three Graces (Hes.
Theog. 945–9). With Anitclia, he had a son, Periphetes, who admittedly was not
described in the most positive way (Apollod. *Bibl.* 3.16.1 describes him harassing
passersby with an iron club while having weak legs himself. He was killed by
Theseus). It should also be acknowledged that from the Classical Period on,
Hephaestus' disability rather rarely appears in iconography. 'Yes, and at Athens
there is a much-praised statue of Vulcan made by Alcamenes, a standing figure,
draped, which displays a slight lameness, though not enough to be unsightly.'
Thus Cicero writes in a chapter in which he claims that anthropomorphic features
of gods are not shared by all peoples (*Nat. D.* 1.83; transl. H. Rackham). Pity for
Hephaestus turns up in various ancient testimonies too, giving possible insights on
people's feelings towards helpless or impaired foundlings (Valerius Flaccus 2.92–
3; see Schmidt 1983–4). Pity or empowerment even lie in the lexicographical
details. In the epics of both Homer (*Iliad* 1.607 and *Od.* 8.300) and Hesiod (*Theog.*
571 and 945), Hephaestus carries the epithet *amphiguēeis*. The old Liddle-Scott-
Jones lexicon translates the term as 'with both feet crooked, lame', while the new
Cambridge Greek Lexicon prefers 'skilled with both hands, ambidextrous',
leaving open the possibility of lameness. Retrospective diagnosis has pointed to
clubfeet for describing Hephaestus' condition. For others, a disease among early
blacksmiths is a more plausible explanation: poisoning due to high concentrations
of arsenic in metal may have caused their suffering. These are likely possibilities,
though far from certainties.

Instead of focusing on either pitying or empowering, it is better to keep in
mind the ambivalence of the character of Hephaestus, fully taking into account
his very diverse functions, which depended on the cultural context. As a lame
god, he could indeed be derided. As a god of technical knowledge, he was
utterly capable of staging his own comic spectacles such as the trapping of

Aphrodite and Ares. As Dionysus' drinking companion, he was closely allied to comic and satyr drama of Athenian festivals. As such, he also became a laughter-inducing character of comic dramas, as in the tradition of padded dancers in comic processions or *kōmoi*. Humour and deriding seem to have been part and parcel of the Hephaestus picture. Commenting on Hephaestus' limping being depicted as comic in the *Iliad*, Lane Fox, abounding in wit, soberly observes: 'Homer's Olympians would find our paralympics hilarious' (2020: 25).

Finally yet importantly, it should be pointed out that, more than any other god, Hephaestus and his disabilities have been the subject of allegorical interpretations. At the heart of these lies Plato's criticism of myth, which explicitly mentions stories such as adulterous Ares and Aphrodite caught by Hephaestus (*Pol.* 3.390b3–c7), or Hephaestus entrapping his mother and being thrown off of Olympus by his father (*Pol.* 2.378d3–e3). According to Plato, all of these allegorical explanations try to come to terms with the deficiencies of the gods being so openly displayed and aim at a higher understanding of the divine. In these traditions, Hephaestus' lameness is explained as the slowness of flames taking possession of the material. Due to his impaired movements, the god needed a staff, symbol of fire needing wood. Hephaestus also is the Demiurge of the perceivable material world, which makes him both a superb creative genius and involved with matters that are by their very nature imperfect. The laughter directed at him should thus be understood as the mocking of the visible world in the Platonic tradition. The allegorical interpretation of Hephaestus was particularly strong in the (Neo)-Platonic and the Stoic tradition and is a remarkable instance of possible discomfort with the representation of a disabled god and a consequent reinterpretation of it.

2.6 Heroes with Mobility Impairment

As was apparent from the stories about Hephaestus, his mobility impairment mostly comes up when it is relevant to the plot. In other instances, it seems of much less importance. Such seems to be the case for other stories too. It is well known how Oedipus as a baby was exposed after his father, Laius, had his ankles pierced – hence he was given the name 'swollen foot' when he eventually came to the house of Polybus, the king of Corinth. One wonders how such injury would have impacted his mobility in later life, yet it is hardly ever spoken about. It is mentioned once as a 'horrible token' he carried with him since he was in infants' swaddles (Soph. *OT* 1035), not exactly what we would consider a mobility impairment. Centuries later, in a parody of tragedy, a satiric writer mentions Oedipus as being *podagros*, suffering from gout (Luc. *Podagra* 255).

Yet this is as far as we get and the theme of Oedipus' reduced mobility is never exploited in ancient literature or iconography.

Mobility impairment did matter in legends, though. Medon was a king of Athens who also became the legendary first archon of the city. Son of King Codrus, he was paralysed (*chōlos*) in one foot. His brother Neileus contested his throne because he did not want Athens to be ruled by a 'cripple'. The matter was brought to the oracle of Delphi. Neileus lost and left for Ionia (Paus. 7.2.1). Here, we are clearly faced with exploitation of an individual's impairment. While political opponents saw it as an impediment for reigning, other Athenians apparently did not share the same view. In this way, Neileus is a forerunner to Roman Sergius Silus (cf. infra p. 36).

The Greek hero Philoctetes is a special case for disabilities in mythology since his impairment turns out to be temporary (Figure 12). Already in the Homeric tradition, he appears as a skilled archer who sailed with his ships

Figure 12 *Philoctetes on the Isle of Lemnus*. Painting by Guillaume Guillon-Lethière (1798) (Louvre, Paris). https://en.wikipedia.org/wiki/Philoctetes#/media/File:Philoctetes_Hermonax_Louvre_G413.jpg

towards Troy. On his way he was bitten by a snake. As the wound caused an unbearable stench his compatriots left him on the isle of Lemnos. Only after ten years did the Greeks decide to get him back since, according to a prophecy, his bow and arrows, which were donated by Heracles, were needed to conquer the city of Troy. According to one tradition – as always, the variety of versions is huge – it was Philoctetes who shot Paris and killed him. He is said to have been one of the few heroes to have made it safely back to his home country, though other traditions situate him in the south of Italy after his return from Troy. The three Athenian tragedians – Aeschylus, Sophocles, and Euripides – all based at least one play on the character, of which only Sophocles' *Philoctetes* survives. In the first century CE, Dio Chrysostom compared the three plays, concluding that he could not decide which one should gain the award for being the best (Dio Chrys. *Or.* 52).

In most versions of the story, Philoctetes is said to have been wounded in his leg, though some writers mention the hand. Sophocles calls Philoctetes 'lame' or 'crippled' on two occasions (*Phil.* 486 and 1032). Tellingly, the tragedian emphasises the undesirable social consequences of Philoctetes' wound: not only the unbearable stench, but also his continuous cry of agony during sacrifice made the Greeks decide to leave him behind on Lemnos (8–11 and 1032–4). Philoctetes himself laments the fact that he was derided because of his 'illness' (257–9), which, according to Dio Chryostom, must have diminished as time passed (*Or.* 52.119). The injury was seen as divine punishment, as the snake was sent by either Hera (Hyg. 102) or Chryse (Soph. *Phil.* 191–200). Full of bitterness and hatred, Philoctetes initially did not want to return to Troy with Neoptolemus and Odysseus, who had taken away his bow with a pretext, abusing their old bonds of guest friendship. He wishes death and ruin to both the Trojans and the Greeks, as well as to himself (*Phil.* 1200–12). Tellingly, in these moments of utter crisis, his foot starts hurting again (1188–9). In the end, only the epiphany of his old friend Heracles (1409–44) manages to persuade Philoctetes to return to Troy. But now, and apparently all of a sudden, his wound is healed. Indeed, in the stories about Philoctetes' role in the siege of Troy or about his safe return to Greece or Italy, there is not one mention of mobility impairment, let alone social isolation. It appears that Philoctetes is able to function well only after he has overcome his pride and bitterness – his trial and suffering appear to have been a personality test. There are remarkable similarities between the Philoctetes tale and the Hephaestus case: Hera's anger, the isle of Lemnos (already in antiquity, Dio Chrys. *Or.* 52.8 remarked that this was not really a deserted place and that Philoctetes must have been helped by inhabitants of the place), being ridiculed and socially isolated, being restituted and allowed to return to one's former status – be it as an Olympian god or as a Greek warrior and hero. The temporary character of the impairment in the case of Philoctetes remains a significant difference, though.

The legend of the Roman hero Gaius Mucius Scaevola is another example of bodily impairment, caused by the loss of the right hand. Already in the days of the Roman Empire, writers considered Scaevola's heroic deed of the year 508 BCE as a miracle, a fabulous story that could hardly be believed were it not that it was documented in the ancient sources and therefore credible (Plut. *Flor.* 4.3 and Plut. *Publ.* 17.1). The most tragic and famous version of the story is found with Livy (2.12–13), who made it a classic in the tales about the Roman striving for freedom in the early days of the Republic. After the expulsion of the last king, Tarquinius Superbus, Rome was besieged by the Etruscan king Porsenna, who wanted to restore the monarchy. This was not anything the young aristocrate Gaius Mucius was prepared to accept. He therefore asked the Senate for permission to go to the enemy's camp since he had a great deed in mind. The senators approved and Mucius set out, hiding a sword under his tunic. Having arrived at the camp he infiltrated the crowd near the royal tribunal. Unfortunately, he was not sure what King Porsenna looked liked, and there was no possibility of asking. Following 'the blind guidance of Fortune', he struck but slew the secretary instead of the king. The royal guards managed to seize him in his flight and dragged him before the king. Unabashed, he announced to the king that the battle against the Romans would be fierce. Porsenna would have to fight for his life from hour to hour. In his anger, the king ordered the prisoner to be burned alive unless he would reveal the details of the plot against him. Mucius was undaunted by the threat and immediately put his right hand in a fire that was kindling on the altar because of a sacrifice. He allowed the hand to burn without showing any sign of pain. After such a stirring deed, Porsenna ordered Mucius set free since he had harmed himself more than his enemy. Mucius boldly replied that he was just the first of 300 young men from Rome who had conspired to attack the king. After the event, Porsenna decided to give up the siege of Rome. Mucius and his progeny from then on proudly bore the name Scaevola ('left hand'), from the heroic loss of his right hand.

The Scaevola tradition resonated far into Roman history in stories about the praetor Marcus Sergius Silus, who, having lost his right hand in the Second Punic War, had gotten it replaced by an iron prosthesis. However, in circa 200 BCE, Silus was debarred by his opponents from performing any sacrifice as a magistrate because of his deformity. An ancestor of Pompey the Great was said to have had his finger burned in the flames of a lamp in front of the Thracian king Genthius without showing any sign of suffering (Val. Max. 3.3.2). The right hand was connected with the cult of the goddess Fides, personification of Faith and Trust. It was with this hand that people swore oaths.

In his comparative study of Indo-European religions, Dumézil's attention was particularly drawn to gods or heroes who had lost their right hand ('the One-Handed'). A striking example is Nuada with the Silver Hand, legendary king of the divine Tuatha Dê Danann tribe of Ireland, who lost his right arm in battle and was succeeded by the beautiful and intelligent Bres of the Fomorian tribe as he could no longer reign with a physical defect. Bres ruled oppressively (the Fomorians had always been the mythological opponents of the people of Ireland). Nuada then became king again after having received a silver prosthesis. Other examples include the Norse god Tyr, whose hand was bitten off since he had put it as a guarantee in the mouth of the evil wolf Fenrir, who was cunningly chained by an unbreakable silk thread; and the Hindu god Savitr, whose two hands were amputated for first sacrifice but replaced by two golden prostheses. Recompensation is key in Dumézil's interpretation. These heroes or gods either gave up on or invested in something essential – in the case of Scaevola, a solemn oath not to be broken. For their sacrifice, they were compensated with special honours or with a prosthesis. The trial of Sergius Silus proves that the apparent consequences of a war wound could function in a rather ambiguous way, though. Though it was an honourable sign, it served in other cases as a way to blame one's political opponent. In the latter case, the disabling effects of a wound are eminently apparent.

3 Other 'Oddities': Monsters, Twins, Dwarfs, and Old Age

In the classification of disabilities that we encountered in Section 1, ethnologists and anthropologists reserved space for a last and 'mixed' category. This not only includes a combination of disabilities of the five former categories, but also entails 'special' cases that were subject to discrimination in certain cultures or environments. For Graeco-Roman mythology, 'monsters' come to mind as a first and rather obvious possibility. Some cultures differentiate between twins. Also here mythology offers interesting cases for antiquity. Dwarfs are another example of possible discrimination. And in the contexts of deities, it may be worth having a brief look at the topic of old age. Were not the immortal gods never supposed ageless? Does this mean that old age by itself was viewed as debilitating?

3.1 Monsters

'Monsters' or extraordinary creatures are at the heart of Greek mythology. Here is what Apollodorus has to say in the very first chapter of his *Library*, in which he largely draws on Hesiod's *Theogony* (who in vv. 139–45 on the Cyclopes and vv. 147–53 on the Hundred-handed has more gruesome details to tell). I underline the cases of extraordinary appearances.

Sky was the first who ruled over the whole world. And having wedded Earth, he begat first the Hundred-handed, as they are named: Briareus, Gyes, Cottus, who were unsurpassed in size and might, each of them having a hundred hands and fifty heads. After these, Earth bore him the Cyclopes, to wit, Arges, Steropes, Brontes, of whom each had one eye on his forehead. But them Sky bound and cast into Tartarus, a gloomy place in Hades as far distant from earth as earth is distant from the sky. And again he begat children by Earth, to wit, the Titans as they are named: Ocean, Coeus, Hyperion, Crius, Iapetus, and, youngest of all, Cronus; also daughters, the Titanides as they are called: Tethys, Rhea, Themis, Mnemosyne, Phoebe, Dione, Thia.

But Earth, grieved at the destruction of her children, who had been cast into Tartarus, persuaded the Titans to attack their father and gave Cronus an adamantine sickle. And they, all but Ocean, attacked him, and Cronus cut off his father's genitals and threw them into the sea; and from the drops of the flowing blood were born Furies, to wit, Alecto, Tisiphone, and Megaera. And, having dethroned their father, they brought up their brethren who had been hurled down to Tartarus, and committed the sovereignty to Cronus. (Apollod. *Bibl.* 1.1; transl. J. G. Frazer)

Apollodorus goes on to tell the well-known story of Cronus being fore-warned that he would be dethroned by his own son, which results in his swallowing Hestia, Demeter, Hera, Pluto, and Poseidon – though Zeus escapes this fate to take over power eventually from his cruel father. In his first chapter, Apollodorus does not even fully exploit the possibilities for a catalogue of monstrosities. In Hesiod, we read that the giants were born from the drops of Cronus' bloody testicles (*Theog.* 185). The Harpies, two-winged women who later became known for snatching away people from the earth, were offspring of the sea god Thaumas and the Oceanid nymph Electra (265–9). Born from the bloody neck-stump of his mother Medusa, herself a monstrous Gorgon, Chrysaor became the father of the three-headed Geryon (287–8). The sea goddess Ceto gave birth to the terrible and violent Echidna, who was not like any mortal or immortal god. She was half a beautiful woman and half an enormous snake (295–304). With the terrible storm-giant Typhon, Echidna had other extraordinary offspring: Orthus, the two-headed, serpent-tailed dog of Geryon; Cerberus, the fearsome dog of the underworld, whose name people hardly dare to mention and who had fifty heads; Hydra, the nine-headed water-serpent from swamps of Lerna; and the three-headed fire-spitting Chimaera (307–25). Out of the incestuous union with her son Orthos came the monstrous and pernicious Sphynx (later depicted with the body of a lion, the head and breast of a woman, wings and sometimes a tail) and the huge Nemean lion (326–32). Another terrible serpent was born from Ceto, this time from the union with her brother Phorcys (333–5).

Regarding this enumeration of monstrous appearances, there are interesting questions to be raised and answered for historians of religion and disabilities. According to Dumézil, enormity and monstrosity play an important role in the fight for sovereignty: first between Uranus and Cronus, then between Cronus and Zeus. After his victory over the Titans, Zeus would use the Hundred-handed as jailors while the Cyclopes fabricated the superior arms with which he won the fight. For their humble yet essential tasks, these creatures were endowed with extraordinary features such as extranumerous limbs or advanced technical skills. They were never represented as 'disabled' in the mythological stories since they were of considerable strength and power.

Very few ancient authors went so far as to deny totally the existence of any of these monstrous creatures. We do find criticism about stories such as the Gigantomachia, in which the Olympian gods fight the giants (Plato, *Rep.* 378 c and Cic. *ND* 2.70). Pausanias found it hard to believe 'that the gods possess any underground dwelling where the souls collect' (transl. W. H. S. Jones and H. A. Ormerod), and he mentions an interpretation by Hecataeus of Miletus that the hound of Hades was merely a poisonous snake which was brought out by Heracles (Paus. 3.25.5). Pausanias, however, was prepared to speculate about the possible existence of a race of giants (8.29.4). He even claims to have seen a Triton among the curiosities at Rome (9.21.1) and theorises about the possibility of a Minotaur, since even in his own times women were known to have given birth to far more extraordinary monsters (1.24.1).

There is little evidence of these extraordinary creatures actually being worshipped. One who was, howeverer, was Cecrops, a king of Athens, who was represented with his lower body part as a snake. As the son of Erechtheus, he was closely connected to the Erechtheion temple on the Acropolis. Sirens appear on Greek archaic tombstones. Winged figures often appear on Etruscan tombs, but it is questionable whether they actually represent the mythical Tages, who sprang out of the ground with the face of a child but with the wisdom of an old sage (Cic. *Div.* 2.50–1). In both the Greek and the Roman traditions, we know of altars and inscriptions for the goddess of Fame and Reputation (Pheme or Fama), but it is mainly the vivid personifications as we find them with poets such as Virgil, Ovid or Valerius Flaccus (first century CE) that stick in the mind. Fama appears as swift-footed and winged – a frightening creature with as many eyes as feathers to her wings, an incredible number of tongues, with noisy mouths that lift up many ears to listen. As a monster, she acts from the sky, preferably by night.

Painters and poets depicted monsters to fit quite various purposes. On Athenian vase paintings from the sixth century BCE on, we see Theseus appearing as the guardian of traditional elite values against those who pervert or threaten them. Outside Attica, he meets and kills Hephaestus' deformed son Periphetes (cf. supra p. 32). Within the boundaries of Attica, he eliminates Scyron, who kicked his visitors over a cliff into the sea where they were devoured by a sea monster. He kills Cercyon, who was known to be excessively strong, and the robber Procrustes, who cut off or stretched out his victims in order to make them fit in his bed. All these 'monstrous' evildoers were viewed as emblems of battle that lacked civilised rules (Pheriphetes), subverters of guest friendship (Scyron), of athletic contest (Cercyon), or of the symposium (Procrustes). In Latin poetry of the Augustan period, more specifically with Ovid and Virgil, monstrosity became an important literary theme, serving various purposes. While feminine monsters such as the Sirens or Medusa are often depicted in a misogynistic way – both enthralling and repulsing the male audience – 'beast men' such as the Minotaur or the centaurs serve more as symbols of the sublime, the hyperbolic, and the innovative – the battle with the giants being one of a conflict of such greatness that it can hardly be contained by Roman epic poems.

A third and final question remains which is of quintessential importance for our focus on the interaction between humans and their mythology. Like most modern languages, ancient Greek and Latin had a somewhat confused terminology for indicating wondrous, strange, or even outrageous appearances or events: ancient authors more than once call the Minotaur, the Cyclopes, or the giants 'monsters'. Often, the vocabulary of the anomalous and of the strange was refined into further categories. Pliny the Elder distinguished between marvels that could possibly characterise individual human beings – such as being exceptionally tall or small, speaking many languages, having incredible sight or hearing (*NH* 7.33–215 somewhat reads like an ancient Guinness Book of Records) – and so-called miraculous human species (*NH* 6.46–52 and 7.6–32). For the latter, we can distinguish between so-called hybrids, with a combination of human and animal parts (for example, the half-human, half-horse centaurs), creatures with one anomalous body part (Cyclopes with one eye), and people with a deviating body size (giants or Pygmies). Could these stories open up possibilities of self-identification by segregated groups? We already encountered the case of individuals labelled as Cyclopes because of their eye defects (cf. supra p. 10). One could also think of a group of dwarfs who had to perform in the battle of the Pygmies against the cranes in a spectacle at the Colosseum staged by Emperor Domitian (Stat. *Silv.* 1.6.57–64). An even more cruel twist to spectacles was given by Commodus. He brought together all men of the City who had lost their feet due to disease or accident. These people were then used in a perverted staging of a fight of Hercules against giants. Their knees were bound together so that they resembled serpents' bodies. They were only allowed to throw sponges instead of stones while the emperor himself, who identified with Hercules, killed them on stage with blows of a club (Cass. Dio 73.20.3). Emperor Heliogabalus was known for keeping a group of *monstra* as pets. His successor, Alexander Severus, wanted to get rid of them in the imperial household. He donated some of them to the people as entertainers while he assigned others to different cities in order to prevent one town from being swamped by beggars (SHA *Alex. Sev.* 34.2). Would these individuals have identified as 'we, the former monsters of Heliogabalus'? Would they have been viewed as such by others? And would theories about monstrous races have been responsible for the fact that some people regarded individuals with (congenital) disabilities as a separate species of man-kind? These are all tantalising possibilities, but it remains difficult to prove any of them.

3.2 Dwarfs

In the common lore of mythology, dwarfs and people of short stature are not infrequently encountered in the Norse tradition, such as the nisse or gnomes. Also the ancient Egyptian pantheon knew the tradition of the 'noble dwarf', a positive figure associated with Horus and Re. This association seems to have disappeared in Egypt from the Hellenistic period on while the dwarf god Bes remained popular in the Graeco-Roman period (Figure 13). In all likelihood, Bes did not belong to the original Egyptian pantheon, though some scholars have claimed that he was a native demon. He seems to have served many quite divergent functions: on amulets, he appears as protector of women and child-birth; he possibly looked after young infants (the so-called kourotrophic func-tion, as on terracottas) and he guarded people during their sleep. He could also function in warfare, as guide of the dead, or in festivals and celebrations. In the Graeco-Roman period, he took on a role as a god of fertility. The many small statuettes of Bes testify to the mixed and ambivalent feelings of people regard-ing malformation: his grotesque and deformed character is depicted by the god's grimace, his protruded tongue, and his leonine or 'black' physiognomics, the latter associated with monkeys or with people from Nubia living in southern Egypt. There are no myths, neither in the Egyptian nor the Graeco-Roman tradition, about Bes, and recent claims that images of him might derive from Down syndrome should be made with due caution. Although there is a likelihood that people recognised similarities between the statuettes and a syndrome that must have occurred very sporadically, such interpretation does not do justice to the many-sided and multifaceted character of Bes's

Figure 13 Amulet of Bes, 1070–712 BCE (Metropolitan Museum of Art, New York City). https://en.wikipedia.org/wiki/Bes#/media/File: Amulet_of_the_God_Bes_MET_DP109383.jpg

iconography. In addition to Bes, Graeco-Roman Egypt was familiar with the legendary geranomachia, the fight between Pygmies and cranes. While partly parodic in character, the confrontation is taken seriously at least by the ancient geographer Pomponius Mela (first century CE), who believed that the Pygmies, farmers who fought the cranes which sought to devour the fruits of their fields, were actually annihilated by these birds (3.81–2). There was indeed a belief among some ancient authors that with the Pygmies a 'race' or 'tribe' of people of small stature existed.

Elsewhere, dwarfs make occasional appearances in Graeco-Roman mythology, as in the case of the Cercopes, two evil highwaymen who harassed travellers (in some versions, there were more of them). In iconography, they sometimes appear with small stature with beards and bulky bodies, and they were in some traditions equated with apes, living caricatures of man (Ov. *Met.* 14.90–100). Their cheating character and their small bodies possibly mirror the dwarfs or *Zwergen* in Germanic folk tradition or the gnomes of Norse lore. Hephaestus was accompanied by creatures of small stature, the Kabeiroi, who were also known for their limp, moving around 'like crabs'; the Daktyls from Crete, whose name implies that they were 'small as a finger'; and the Telchines from Rhodes or Crete – all these 'small demons' of Hephaestus sometimes have physical appearances that suggest characteristics of dwarfs. To these may be added his servant Cedalion, who helped him at his forge on Lemnos. In the second half of the second century CE, Lucian describes an ancient painting that depicts the blind giant Orion carrying Cedalion on his shoulder, who shows Orion the way to the sunlight. Viewing the scene and possibly giving instructions to the pair is Hephaestus (Lucian, *De domo* 28–9). A Puglian amphora from Foggia even depicts Hephaestus himself as a dwarf at the moment he is about to set free his mother, Hera, whom he had bound to a magic throne (Figure 14).

This evidence combined does not allow for either a conclusively positive or a negative judgement on the role of dwarfs in Graeco-Roman mythology – let alone in society. Aristotle pointed to the 'inferior intellect' of people of small stature (*Part. an.* 686b23–7). Scholars of ancient mentality and ideas such as Geoffrey Lloyd have pointed to the constant intermingling of science, folklore, and ideology. In the case of dwarfs, similarities are perceived between small children and animals, both of which do not excel in intellect and are known for their 'hesitating' or even 'creeping' movements. While it is true that people of small stature are often depicted as making their way in

Figure 14 Amphora from Foggia. Apulian red-figure amphora with small-figured Hephaestus with axe and Hera on the throne (Foggia, Museo Civico). https://gantzmythsources.libs.uga.edu/p-76-with-art

society – even performing useful jobs – depreciation of their physical appearance and intellectual or moral capacities always lurks in the background. On one archaic Latin inscription from Praeneste, dated to the fourth century BCE, the god Castor is mentioned as 'father of the dwarfs' (*pater poumilionom*; *CIL* 14.4110). We sadly have no idea what this short text could hint at. More explicit, though, is an extract from an astrological calendar on a Greek papyrus from the second century CE: 'The god causes extreme old age, until (a man) is bent by old age; he causes humps or makes (men) bent by disease; he causes dwarfs to be born, and monsters (*terata*) similar to beetles, and people who have no eyes, who are like a beast, who have difficulty speaking, and are deaf, and toothless' (*P. Oxy.* 3.465).

Here, we are projected back to the 'monsters' (teratology). The fragment recalls Roman accounts on markets of bizarre appearances (Plut. *De curiositate* 520c). Deformity and extravagance indeed seem to have been popular during the Roman Empire. It is only fair to consider at least how this would have caused individuals of small stature to identify with mythological dwarfs.

3.3 Twins

Scholars of comparative religion and mythology have long recognised the importance of twins and multiplets. On one hand, they serve as symbols of complementarity, fertility, prosperity, and abundance. On the other, they may be viewed as the product of maternal infidelity, illegitimacy, stain, a bad omen, and even disturbance of the cosmic order. The negative interpretation opens the possibility of a 'disabling' effect. Anthropologists and ethnologists too have pointed to the potential disadvantage of being twins in certain cultures: exposure of both infants or the one who was considered the weaker, the 'evil' or 'weaker one' as the antagonist to his brother in later life; childbirths in which one of the twins died (the surviving one was called Vopiscus, but Pliny the Elder ranks such instances among the very rare cases that he considers 'miracles'; see *NH* 7.47).

Graeco-Roman mythology abounds with examples of twins. Surveys have listed more than fifty instances of pairs of twins, who are often well attested both in the literary and the iconographic source material. Some of them belong to the best-known mythological histories of the Graeco-Roman world.

Heracles' remarkable virility came to light when he was only eighteen years old. During his visit to King Thespius, who had invited him to come and kill the lion of Cithaeron, the king ordered his fifty daughters to go to bed with the hero. They all did, in one and the same night, according to Pausanias, in five or fifty consequent nights in the version of authors with more sense of reality. The ancient authors agree that Heracles accomplished his mission quite well: all daughters got pregnant and gave birth, while the eldest got twins – as did the youngest, according to Pausanias (9.27.6–7, compare with Apollod. *Bibl.* 2.7.8). Quite unsurprisingly, such tales of hypersexuality were eagerly dished up by biographers of supposedly 'bad' and unrestrained Roman emperors, such as the usurper Proculus (r. 281), who had sex with 10 captive women in one night and with 100 in the space of fifteen days (Historia Augusta, *Firm., Sat, Proc. et Bonos.* 12.7). Be this as it may, in the case of Heracles, we never hear of the two mothers with twins being treated differently than their other – admittedly also fertile – sisters. Twins appear in ancient myths too. Leto gave birth to Apollo and Artemis on the isle of Delos while fleeing from jealous Hera, who could not bear the fact that Leto was pregnant by her husband, Zeus. Also, after their birth, Hera continued to persecute Leto and her children. However, the fact that they were twins does not really seem to have had an impact on Hera's anger. In addition, Heracles and his twin brother, Iphicles, came close to being killed right after their birth. It was again Hera, who had sent a snake in order to kill the babies. The infant Heracles immediately grasped the opportunity of demonstrating both his enormous bodily strength and his protective attitude towards Iphicles, which he would show in later life too. Also here, Hera's anger is not sparked by Alcmene's being the mother of twins, but by Zeus's infidelity in fathering Heracles and so engendering a twin to Iphicles, his half-brother: Zeus had approached Alcmene in the guise of her lawful husband, Amphitryon, with the result that she was impregnated by two different future fathers. Twinhood is associated with perversion of the biological order in the case of Spartan queen Leda's impregnation by Zeus in the guise of a swan. Out of an egg, or different eggs (again the versions vary), came the Dioscuri – the brothers Castor and Polydeuces (Pollux) – and also – at least in some traditions – Helena and Clytemnaestra. Also here, superfecundation plays a role, Castor being the human son of Leda's husband, Tyndaraeus, and Polydeuces being the immortal son of Zeus. As protective demigods, the two brothers were important in the Roman legends too – there is again no indication of a disabling consequence of being twins while the alternation between death (mortality) and life (immortality) may be at stake here. Almost ten mythological twins are said to have been exposed. Young Melanippe was impregnated by Poseidon, gave birth in solitude, and exposed her twin sons, Boeotus and Aeolus, who were in one version nourished by a cow, in other versions found by a shepherd or adopted by a childless couple. Antiope, also seduced by a god, gave birth to her twins, Amphion and Zethus. She abandoned the children on Mount

Cithaeron, but a shepherd found them. Only as young men would they be reunited with their mother. The combination of being twins by a god and a human mother, exposed, breastfed by a she-wolf, found by a shepherd, and reunited with the mother as young men also occurs in the famous Roman myth about Rhea Silvia, made pregnant by Mars and the mother of Romulus and Remus, who stood at the origin of the City of Rome. The rivalry between the two brothers and the consequent fratricide seems rather exceptional in the mythical repertoire on twins, who were mostly known for their solidarity and mutual support. In the Old Testament, we have the case of Isaac and Esau as another instance of rivalry between twins, though this did not lead to fratricide.

To conclude, there seems to be no evidence of twins being at a disadvantage *because of* their being twins. Greek and Roman cultures seem to have been rather favourable to the phenomenon of twinhood, though admittedly some stories about them are connected with life-threatening conditions or mothers being in danger because of irregular pregnancy.

Monstrosity brings us to instances of twinhood that come close to disabilities. The Aloades, sons of Poseidon and Iphimedia, grew up to become giants whose *hybris* and aggression eventually turned against Olympus, for which Apollo killed them. Agrius and Oreius were born from the union of Polyphonte with a bear. Again they became aggressive giants and brigands, who were eventually punished by Zeus and turned into birds. The Molionidae, warrior-twins born out of an egg, are already mentioned in the *Iliad*, without the mention of a physical anomaly. Later tradition states that they only had one body, with four feet, four arms and two heads – such representation is strongly present in the iconographical tradition of the Geometric Period. Here, one may also think of the monstrous three-bodied Geryon. Also female twinhood, a rare occurrence in ancient myths, is sometimes connected to a hybrid appearance: Gorgones, Harpies, and Erinyes come to mind. Surely in the case of the Molionidae and Geryon, we may think of Siamese twins, who are also listed as monstrous prodigies in the *Liber Prodigiorum* by Julius Obsequens (fourth or fifth century). In some circumstances, their birth was viewed as endangering the community – a pollution that required immediate cleansing by their elimination. The actual situation and the interpretation of it no doubt also had on impact on triplets or the birth of even more children at the same time. Again, the reception of such phenomenon did not need to be negative. For Roman myths, Dionysus of Halicarnassus (*c.*60 BCE–after 9 CE) mentions the birth of triplets in Rome and Alba Longa, respectively the Horatii and the Curiatii, as extraordinary 'events' promising prosperity and happiness to their communities (*Ant. Rom.* 3.13.3–4). Just as the twins Romulus and Remus, the Horatii triplets, with their victory over the Curiatii, belong to the foundation myths of the City of Rome.

3.4 Old Age

As we have seen in this Element, gods are born, though we seldom hear about their infant years and how they looked physically. It seems as if they were born immediately in full adult shape. Zeus, however, was nurtured and guarded as a baby by the Curetes. Dionysus, about whom we are told that he was taken out of the body of his immolated mother, Semele, was born from the thigh of Zeus and then raised as a little boy by the nymphs of Mount Nysa. We also read about deities being wounded in battle and being emotionally or physically hurt. But since they were immortal, basically not a single god would die. This also means that gods could not take away their own lives or grow older (cf. supra p. 10). Though both Uranus and Cronus were forced into retirement (the Egyptian upper-god Ra famously decided about this himself when he felt he was getting older), and though Cronus later on is often seen as an aged god, there are very few instances of ageing gods in Graeco-Roman mythology (but note *Hymn. Hom.* 5.244–6 on gods dreading old age). As we have seen, old age was a condition unknown to the golden race, the first race of human beings, while the fifth race would one day be born with grey hair in their temples – a sign of their forthcoming doom (cf. supra p. 12). On the other hand, the old-aged sea god Oceanus was highly respected: 'and straight went down to Tethys, venerable goddess of the sea, and to old Ocean, whom oft the gods hold in reverence' (Ovid, *Met.* 2.509–11).

Just as there was Hebe, goddess of youth and cupbearer to the gods (it is not entirely sure whether the personified Iuventas worshipped by the Romans was actually the same figure; see Cic. *Ad Att.* 1.18.3), there existed a god of old age named Geras or Senectus. It is not too difficult to describe this deity and the representations of him in a few words: poor, hideous, loathsome, wearying, and dreaded. In iconography, he appears emaciated and grotesque, with swollen genitals. He was said to be the son of the dark Nyx (Night), who begot him without the presence of a father (Hes. *Theogn.* 211–25). No wonder that he was not really worshipped. The mention of an altar and possibly a cult of him at Gades belongs to the sphere of eccentricity of a people also known to be excessive in religion by having shrines to Penia (Poverty) and Techne (Craft) (Philostr. *VA* 5.4.167).

Mythology, on one hand, is full of fearsome creatures sometimes depicted as old and haggard: Charon the ferryman of the underworld, Fates, Furies, and

Graeae. On the other hand, longevity was a feature that could contribute to respectability for Homeric figures such as Nestor, the king of Pylos; Laertes, the king of Ithaca and father of Odysseus; or Anchises, a Trojan and the father of Aeneas (Figure 15). The case of the seer Teiresias has already been mentioned. The marginality of old age put aged individuals on the same level as women and children – their physical weakness required especial attention from the supernatural and made them more likely to be in touch with the divine world. As such, old age in certain cases and with certain individuals did not necessarily have a disabling effect. It all depended very much on the given circumstances.

Rejuvenation and the desire for it is a folktale motif in many cultures, and from early Greek literature on we read about elderly people wanting to scrape their old age from them as snakes shed their skins. Tithonus became the proverbial figure for this desire. As the mortal lover of Eos, the goddess of the dawn, he asked for immortality, but without thinking about eternal youth to accompany it. With age increasing, he shrivelled away and was released from his long decrepitude only when he became a cicada. Ancient medical writers

Figure 15 Anchises. *Aeneas Carrying Anchises*. Painting by Charles André van Loo (1729) (Paris, Louvre). https://de.wikipedia.org/wiki/Anchises#/media/ Datei:Eneasanquises.jpg

dish up the remarkable story of a sophist who at age forty published a book on how to remain forever young and avoid the undesirable effects of old age. By the time he had reached age eighty, his public appearance was subject to general mockery, at which point he revised his book by claiming that only very few people could actually avoid the effects of old age and that one should start earlier than he himself had done. He now was prepared to offer his services to whomever wanted to start early enough and pay for it (Gal. *De san. tuenda* 1.12 and 6.3). This remarkable anecdote probably mirrors desires as those of Tithonus expressed in myths and folktales.

4 Purity and Wholesomeness for Priests and Cultic Servants?

4.1 The Requirement of Able Bodies and Its Relativity

Both disability with the occasional recovery from it and 'odd' appearances were part and parcel of Greek and Roman tales, legends, and myths. But should not such phenomena be kept away, as far as possible, from the sphere of religion in its widest sense: from performers of ritual, from cultic objects, and sacrificial animals, and maybe even from the worshippers? Did priests in antiquity need to be perfect? This is at least the impression one gets when reading statements as the following:

> A priest must be without defect . . . A priest whose body has a blemish is to be avoided like something of ill omen. This is an object of censure even in sacrificial victims: how much more in priests! Once a man becomes priest, more careful watch must be paid for any disability; if a priest is maimed, the gods must be angry. (Sen. *Controv.* 4.2; transl. M. Winterbottom)

The controversy is about the high priest Lucius Caecilius Metellus, who rescued the Palladium from the temple of Vesta during a fire in 241 BCE. As he had seen a sacred object he was not supposed to set his eyes on, he was punished with blindness. The story about his punishment belongs to the sphere of the legendary and it is not sure whether the Roman readers of Seneca the Elder (*c.*54 BCE –*c.*39 CE) believed it had ever taken place. Indeed, the fragment quoted is part of a declamation exercise in a school of the rhetors, where students were taught how to argue both for and against. We also read arguments in favour of Metellus. His blinding made him even greater as a priest, and the Vestals should be glad to have had him. Without him their whole temple and the worship of Vesta would have been destroyed. The law on perfect priests – which in reality did not exist; it was only formulated for the sake of this declamation – applied to the priest's mindset and mentality, not to his body. It was a requirement for entering the priesthood, not for those who already held it.

It is nevertheless interesting to notice that a defect or disability might be used against someone performing religious duties. Unlike many cultures in the ancient Mediterranean world, Greeks and Romans did not have a separate class of priests. At least in the West of the Roman Empire, priests were essentially magistrates. The profession was never considered a vocation. They were supposed to observe scrupulously the performative character of the ritual and were ideally of bodily and moral soundness and integrity. This is strongly emphasised in Plato's *Laws*:

> As to the priests, we shall entrust it to the god himself to ensure his own good pleasure, by committing their appointment to the divine chance of the lot; but each person who gains the lot we shall test, first, as to whether he is sound and true-born, and secondly, as to whether he comes from houses that are as pure as possible, being himself clean from murder and all such offences against religion, and of parents that have lived by the same rule. (Pl. *Leg.* 6.759c; transl. L. G. Bury)

Apart from Plato, there is a long Greek tradition in literary texts and inscriptions on the approbation (*dokimasia*) of priests, kings, and magistrates, for whom bodily health and bodily integrity (*hygiēs* and *holoklēros*) were key features. In the wake of this, scholars of Roman religion, among whom no one less than Georg Wissowa (1859–1931) have claimed that the same requirement existed in Roman religion. However, on the face of it, only three texts point to the necessity of physical wholeness for Roman priests. One is mainly of antiquarian interest, dealing with the archaic priesthood of the *flamines curiales* (Dion. Hal. *Ant.* 2.21). The second is about Vestal Virgins who enter the order, but it is completely silent about what happened in case of a defect acquired later on (Gell. *NA* 1.12). The third passage rather relates to augurs. While it explicitly mentions the necessity of both priests and victims being pure, intact, and sound, its remarks on augurs and a temporary impediment again point to a rather specific context and situation more than to a general rule (Plut. *Quaest. Rom.* 73).

A definite sense of pragmatism seems to have been the explanation for the requirement of perfect bodies. For priests or magistrates who performed cultic duties, we have plenty of examples of adjustments to particular situations. Here one can think of another Metellus, from the third or second century BCE, known as the tongue-tied pontifex, consul, and holder of the triumph, who prepared for several months when he was charged with speaking out the words for a temple's dedication (cf. supra p. 27). We already met the war hero Sergius Silus, whose war wound and consequent prosthesis were used by his opponents to debar him from performing the sacred rites. He was never forced to resign, though, and he carried on performing religious duties during his praetorship. Publius Vatinius had been praetor and consul and was admitted to the college of augurs while he was at the same time unmercifully mocked by his opponents such as Cicero because of his goitres and gout. Despite his defects from early age on, the later Emperor Claudius was appointed an augur by Augustus himself (Suet. *Claud*. 4). The same pragmatism must have applied to sacrificial animals and the audience. One can hardly expect the whole crowd attending sacrifice to be of sound health – some symptoms were interpreted as disturbing or distressing, though, such as epileptic seizures or a mad man's behaviour (according to Theophr. *Char*. 16.14, the superstitious man spits in his lap when confronted with these; see also the requirement of performing sacrifice with clean hands, already with Hes. *Op*. 725, with further requirements for cleanness in *Op*. 727–35). As for victims of sacrifice, blemishes could indeed be interpreted as a bad omen, but again such interpretations were often ad hoc and bad signals could of course be ignored.

4.2 Why Purity and Wholesomeness?

There are different reasons for the stress on purity and wholesomeness where religious matters and duties are concerned. No doubt moral qualification played an important role. For this the ancient ideal of *kalokagathia* was perfectly applicable: bodily perfection reflected the qualities of the soul and character; those who look good and perfect were considered good and perfect. In the same way, the Latin *vitium* means both a defect and a vice/fault. The aesthetic criterion is an explanatory factor too, since anything that was culturally viewed as unpleasant or asymmetric to the senses needed to be held far away from the sphere of most religious practices (though not from all, since there are also examples of obscene rites in order to provoke fertility). The pragmatic-functional criterion is a third explanation. One would have not have wanted a priest to stammer when reciting the holy texts, while in certain situations blindness or deafness would be impairing factors too.

Such beliefs and attitudes have played a role in many religious traditions throughout the world. They are eminently present with an eclectic and non-specialist author such as Pliny the Elder. In his *Natural History*, he sticks to the view that beauty is to be found in every single detail of nature, even in small animals such as insects, which are at first sight not worth studying. His views were inspired by writers such as Aristotle (*Part. An*. 1.5, 645a), writers who focus on beauty and harmony in the cosmos that constitutes nature. Thus earth (*terra mater*) is basically kind and indulgent, an emanation of the goodness of nature itself (Plin. *HN* 2.155). Now this harmony and beauty should be reflected in our religious practice too. Human beings mediate religion through their bodies: suppliants touch the ground with their knees (*HN* 11.250). In the same way, other body parts have religious meaning too: right hands, chins, earlobes, and mouths (*HN* 28.135). 'Life is upheld by religion.' Therefore, healthy and wholesome body parts are in place for performing right and dignified rituals. Here, a comparison formulated by Pliny is revealing. After all, we do not pour libations to the gods ' with wines from a vine that has not been pruned, from one that has been struck by lightning, or one in the neighbourhood of which a man has been hanged, or wine made from grapes that have been trodden out by someone with sore feet' (*HN* 14.119; transl. H. Rackham).

There seems to be an inherent tension between viewing divinely inspired nature as holy, sound, and perfect on one hand, and coping with the contrast of the real world on the other. In the real world, imperfection and irregularity inevitably belong to the daily life of priests, worshippers, and sacrifice.

5 The Role of Christianity and Monotheism

There are several good reasons for including a section on Christianity in an Element on Greek and Roman mythology. First, in more than one way, Graeco-Roman gods and heroes and their stories never died. Up to very late antiquity and into the era we commonly call the Middle Ages, we hear of bans and interdictions regarding pagan beliefs, customs, and festivals. The transition to the new religion was always gradual, and Christians incorporated many elements of pagan religion, not seldom replacing deities by saints, in sanctuaries that kept their functions for healing. Second, for Christian thinkers and writers, mythological stories and allusions were often there at the background too. Mythology kept on being part and parcel of their education, and the way they discussed and contrasted it with Christian faith can be revealing for how they saw their own religion as fundamentally different from what came before them. No one has put it more saliently than St Jerome (342/7–420), in an image full of aggressive appropriation: 'If you want to marry a captive, you must first shave her head and eyebrows, shave the hair on her body and cut her nails, so must it be done with profane literature, after having removed all that was earthly and idolatrous, unite with her and make her fruitful for the Lord' (Jer. *Ep.* 83; transl. Morales 2007: 66).

Third, with the many healing miracles, performed by Jesus himself in the tradition of the Old Testament Messianic prophecies on the healing of the blind, deaf, lame, and mute (*Is* 35:5–6), and continued by the apostles and the saints, disability and recovery from it stood at the core of Christian religion. Even more so: the Son of God himself went through atrocious suffering and bore its marks on his resurrected body. Fourth, we should consider the Christian eschatological tradition, with its emphasis on the resurrection of perfect bodies at the Final Day of Judgement and the imagery of damned bodies and eternal suffering in hell, with apocalyptic tours of hell going back to the second half of the second century CE. Such Christian 'mythology' at least had the potential of impacting views on (dis)ability, healing, and health.

5.1 Christian Criticism of Graeco-Roman Mythology and the Role of Disability

As for the Christian criticism of traditional pagan polytheism, it should be stressed first and foremost that a great deal of the traditional denunciation goes back a very long time in antiquity. Indeed, the quest for a more purified religion, taking away the blemishes of anthropomorphic interpretations of the divine, starts in the sixth century BCE with the critique of writers such as Hecataeus of Miletus. Their arguments have been developed in Section 1 and there is no need to repeat them here. But it is good to realise that godly infirmity and disability play only a very minor part in them. While Christian authors too could have potentially elaborated strongly on the absurdity of worshipping disabled gods, they only do so very rarely. In a certain sense, and though they would not admit it themselves, there is a certain similarity between pagan critics of the so-called *theologia mythica* such as the learned Varro (116–27) or the critically sceptic Cicero in his treatises on religion on one hand, and church fathers like Tertullian or Augustine on the other. What mostly mattered to the pagan writers was the philosophical truth, which was hidden in traditional religion. To this Christian writers add the absurdity of the fragmentation of divine power in polytheism. They focus on the inescapable truth of monotheism. What follows is a key passage from the *Roman Antiquities* by Dionysius of Halicarnassus about the reign of King Romulus and his approach to religion:

> But he rejected all the traditional myths concerning the gods that contain blasphemies or calumnies against them, looking upon these as wicked, useless (*anōpheleis*) and indecent, and unworthy, not only of the gods, but even of good men; and he accustomed people both to think and to speak the best of the gods and to attribute to them no conduct unworthy of their blessed nature ... Indeed, there is no tradition among the Romans either of Caelus being castrated by his own sons or of Saturn destroying his own offspring to secure himself from their attempts or of Jupiter dethroning Saturn and confining his own father in the dungeon of Tartarus, or, indeed, of wars, wounds (*traumata*), or bonds of the gods, or of their servitude among men ... Let no one imagine, however, that I am not sensible that some of the Greek myths are useful to mankind, part of them explaining, as they do, the works of Nature by allegories, others being designed as a consolation for human misfortunes, some freeing the mind of its agitations

and terrors and clearing away unsound opinions, and others invented for
some other useful purpose. But, though I am as well acquainted as anyone
with these matters, nevertheless my attitude toward the myths is one of
caution, and I am more inclined to accept the theology of the Romans, when
I consider that the advantages from the Greek myths are slight and cannot be
of profit to many, but only to those who have examined the end for which
they are designed; and this philosophic attitude is shared by few. The great
multitude, unacquainted with philosophy, are prone to take these stories
about the gods in the worse sense and to fall into one of two errors: they
either despise the gods as buffeted by many misfortunes, or else refrain from
none of the most shameful and lawless deeds when they see them attributed
to the god. (Dion. Hal. *Ant. Rom.* 2.18–20; transl. E. Carey)

Apart from the preference for 'the theology of the Romans', Christian authors
would agree with this criticism of Greek mythology and even resort to similar
arguments in order to rebuke it. And yet only two words possibly point to what
we would call disabled gods: it may be implied in the Greek term denoting
'uselessness' and there is the reference to wounding.

A same similarity is noticeable in criticism of monsters and extraordinary
creatures. As we have seen in Section 3, pagan writers sometimes ridiculed the
belief in them and tried to rationalise the topic by turning to geographical
(ethnographical), historicising, or allegorical explanations. On the other hand,
they tended to confirm the existence of at least some 'monsters', pointing to
findings of excavated bones or actual eyewitnesses. As can be expected,
Christian writers exploited the occurrence of extraordinary creatures in Graeco-
Roman myths in order to ridicule pagan beliefs. Sirens, Titans, and giants were
among their favourite subjects of mockery, as were the hybrid Egyptian gods,
who were equalled to demons. In much the same way as pagan writers, they also
turned to allegoric interpretations of such creatures. And yet at the same time,
they believed that some 'monsters' actually existed. Jerome mentions how the
monk Paul, at the age of 113, on his way to visit his younger fellow monk
Anthony, crossed the path of a hippocentaur. Jerome is eager to point out to his
readers that a similar creature had actually been seen and put on display in
Alexandria during the reign of Constantius II (337–61 CE). After his death, this
hippocentaur was conserved in salt, transported to Antiochia, and seen by the
emperor himself (*vit. Paul.* 7–8). St Augustine believed that the giants had
actually existed before the times of the flood. For his own day, he accepts the
existence of all sorts of hybrids and 'monsters', for which he refers to hermaph-
rodites or prodigious births. In one way or another, often not understood by
men, these creatures belong to the plan God has for the world (August. *De civ.
D.* 16.8). Also, Christian writers have spilt gallons of ink denouncing the pagan
worship of images and statues representing gods. Here, their main objection is

the anthropomorphism, which they rebuke with arguments that remind us of pagan predecessors such as Heraclitus and Xenophanes. They also rage against the veneration of statues as if the divine powers were present in the objects themselves, while it turned out that they were in actual fact completely power-less: they have hands but they cannot touch, they have feet but cannot walk, and they do not speak in spite of having a mouth (*Ps* 113:15 – see also *Sap* 13). Again the representation of a deity with wounds or a disability does not play any role in the fierce polemics against the veneration of statues and images – the pagan belief in the existence of hybrid statues, semi-human and semi-animal, was an element of criticism, though.

5.2 Attention to 'Categories' of Disabled and a Wounded or Disabled Christian God?

In the miracles of Jesus, disability played a key role. In more than one way, miracles caused certain disabilities to be categorised: the blind, the deaf, the mute, the lame, and the leprous – to whom should be added the possessed, a tradition of healing being largely alien to Graeco-Roman customs. In the wake of Jesus, the apostles and the saints would repeat these miracles for centuries to come. Unlike mythological stories, these healing miracles were set in historical times, often with minute details about context, witnesses, and names and symptoms of the ones who received healing. Mythological stories and healing miracles do have important things in common, though. They play a vital role in anchoring the value system of a society and affirmatively provide answers people sought to persistent questions regarding their human existence. Telling and retelling such stories time and again reminded audiences and congregations of Jesus' healing powers, surely when the telling was done in a ritual context. The occurrence of these stories raised questions about the need for charity, the tension between the high-pitched ideal of equality and the ways of the real world, or the existential question of why some receive healing and others do not and why the one and only God, who is good by definition, would ever allow suffering. For the question of healing, issues of moral responsibility and per-sonal belief come in too.

The biblical tradition has even more potential for another approach to disability. In the Judaic belief, with its hostility towards anthropomorphic representations of God, it would come as a surprise to depict Yahweh as sick, infirm, or somehow disabled. Yet it sometimes happens in strong imagery, as when Yahweh as an avenger declares how he will be moth to Ephraim and rot to the house of Judah (*Hos* 5:12). Also, the suffering Servant of Yahweh is the opposite of the beautiful human form one would expect: 'As many were astonished at you; his appearance was so marred, beyond human semblance, and his form beyond that of the children of mankind' (*Isa* 52:14).

From its very beginnings, Christianity also had the potential of taking a different stance toward the Graeco-Roman ideal of *kalokagathia*, pointing to bodily and moral perfection. Not only did the Son of God go through the most degrading and mutilating torture, also the thirteenth apostle, Paul, mentions his own 'weakness' (*astheneia*) more than once (2 *Cor* 10:10, 12:7–10; *Gal* 4:13). Jesus himself broke with scapegoat mechanisms and concepts of guilt as it relates to disability by saying that it was not the congenitally blind man or his parents who had sinned against God (*Joh* 9:1–3). And Jesus' resurrected body bears scars or wounds to demonstrate 'stability' of identity, as is clear from his invitation to Thomas to touch them (*Joh* 20:24–7).

5.3 Christian Eschatology and a New 'Underworld' of Disabled Bodies

Already in the second and third century, Christian notions of the resurrected body intersected with the concept of heavenly healing. There needs to be a continuity between the earthly and the resurrected body in order for us to be recognisable as individuals in the afterlife. At the same time, Christian writers believed in an eschatological cleansing. In Christian eschatological thought, all will be resurrected with perfect bodies, as bodily or mental imperfections do not constitute who people essentially are in the eyes of God. No deformity or infirmity will exist anymore. Limbs will be reattached, but the scars will rather be pleasant tattoos. The two sexes will continue to exist, though (August. *De civ. D.* 22.15–22).

Apparently, this notion of cleansing reveals a tension. Already very early in Christianity, concepts of ancient aesthetics began to play their role. The white robes of the martyrs in the *Apocalypse*, indicating purity and beauty, are an example of this (6:11). Those who receive the mark of the beast, on the contrary, accept a 'painful and foul-smelling wound' (16:2; transl. C. Moss). Throughout the *Revelation*, the good are depicted as beautiful while the damned appear hideous and ugly. The Christian iconographical representation of saints in heaven is one of symmetry and serene radiance too. Here, the Graeco-Roman ideal of *kalokagathia* seems to be back fully.

To this should be added the apocalyptic tours of hell, extra-canonical texts which gained considerable popularity with Christians from the second half of the second century on, in diverse language traditions. In depicting eternal suffering and torture for the condemned, the apocalyptic writers were keen on pointing out why sinners ended up like this: failure to care for the poor; sexual transgressions such as homosexuality, adultery, or incest; lack of care for one's household (including abortion or exposure of infants) – they were all considered good and just reasons to assign people to suffering. No doubt such suffering was perceived as 'real' by the audience of these days. There was no question of symbolic interpretation of it. Blindness and eternal darkness, amputated limbs, eternal weeping, fire, worms, or gnashing teeth belonged to the repertoire of eternal condemnation. At the background were deeply rooted ideas about the inferiority of the female gender, the superiority of the active over the passive, and the undesirability of the black colour, including in skin. Christian hell was an underworld fundamentally different from the Greek Hades, where punishments were initially reserved for occasional and exceptional transgressive wrongdoers such as the Corinthian king Sisyphus, who had tried to cheat Death; the Lydian king Tantalus, who had stolen divine nectar and ambrosia after a meal with the gods; or the Titan Prometheus, who took way fire from heaven and brought it to the humans. Occasional sinners are prominent in Vergil's in book 6 of the Aeneid too. Christian hell on the contrary fixed norms and marked those who deviated from them. It is therefore right to call the bodies of these condemned 'disabled'. They deviated physically, morally, and ethically from what had been set out as normative.

Conclusion: Disability As Anachronism or Analogy?

Ancient Myths As Emancipatory Stories for the Disabled?

How can ancient myths be helpful for issues such as the integration of people with disabilities into present-day society? To this question, an anonymous author on the *We Capable* website has a clear and outspoken answer, at least as concerns myths from Hindu mythology.[3] Let there be no doubt that the answer is a definitely positive one. In short and salient stories, nicely illustrated with colourful drawings, we are offered a compilation of nine different characters of Indian myths. They are all there: a 'monster' with no fewer than eight deformities in his body; a blind king; a villain with a limp and a malformed eye; an author with intellectual disability; a maid and a lady with a hunchback and blindness in one eye; and a blind poet.

The amount of Vedic and Sanskrit literature is enormous, and it has been estimated that a large bulk of it has never been properly published in scholarly editions with commentaries and translations – at least in the Western contemporary world, where chairs of Sanskrit and Indian studies have largely been abandoned and are sadly regarded as relics of old-fashioned orientalism. Contrary to this, classicists and ancient historians find themselves in a privileged position. In writing this Cambridge Element, I could rely on

---

[3] https://wecapable.com/disability-indian-mythology.

a scholarly tradition that goes back approximately 150 years (the oldest item in the bibliography dates from 1894 and I respectfully acknowledge that the wealth of detail it contains makes it remarkably up to date and fit for research). Based on such rich material, the scholar of antiquity will face no difficulty at all in drawing a parallel list to the *We Capable* Indian examples. Admittedly, a parallel for the intellectual impairment seems challenging – but here, the Indian example does not seem to be crystal clear either, and the help of the Egyptian deity Bes might be called in to fill the gap, as I explained in Section 2. Also, with the aid of some rhetorics and aptly attractive illustrations, a classicist will have little difficulty in demonstrating how all the disabled Greek and Roman gods or heroes were 'fully' integrated into the society to which they belonged. In the end, such is hardly surprising. Anthropologists have repeatedly pointed out how the community concept is something that distinguishes present-day Western approaches towards disability from other time periods and cultures, while, according to Michel Foucault, it is the medicalised approach of the nineteenth century that separated the 'abled' from the 'disabled'.

But should such observations be a reason for optimism regarding the premodern past as a much better place for the disabled? I feel this would be making the sources tell what they actually never say. Coming to terms with the difficulty and challenges caused by an infirmity, trying to give it a sense, and making the best out of it seems a much better description. There is not one single ancient text that claims that Teiresias was an exceptionally gifted seer *because* of his blindness. Blindness was his punishment and divine lore was a compensation for the visual impairment. Hephaestus was a gifted artisan and a god who played a major role in the Graeco-Roman pantheon, *despite* his limp and possible hunchback. There is hardly anything positive in famous literary depictions of Oedipus' blindness, Thersites' ridiculed walk, Philoctetes' war wound, the personification of Plutus as blind and poor, or the deeply touching cases of war trauma with agents and victims of the Trojan war. Roman legends of war veterans also pointed to possible adverse or hostile reactions regarding their wounds. As for 'monsters' and creatures that were sensed as odd, they indeed appear as fully able, strong, and to be reckoned with in battles and wars, but again their existence never gave rise to the celebration of diversity that readers of nowadays sometimes tend to see in it.

Ancient Myths As Stories Pernicious to the Disabled? Blaming Classical Civilisation for Ableism?

'Warning. Reflections in the mirror may be distorted by exposure to corporate pop culture and its stereotypes about beauty.' The advert almost literally stared at me while I was considering the final section of this Element. I could not have come across it at a better moment. In more than one way, it catches what needs to be said about (im)perfect bodies in classical culture and about how people have dealt with them throughout the centuries.

My personal historical interests have never been confined to the ancient world. As such, I very much like visits to museums that focus on the contemporary world, say, the history of a country after the Second World War. Such exhibits broaden one's views on antiquity too. They show time and again how rapid technological development, sophisticated medicine, worldwide mobility, and emancipatory movements have changed our lives in such a way that it has become difficult to empathise with people who lived in one's own region, say, one century before. It is exactly these changes and developments that have fundamentally altered the way we look at bodily (dis)ability too.

Identity and the idea of belonging is a perfect example of this. Rapid information, communication, and internet connectivity mean that one can relate with others all over the world and create one's own community. In the context of disabilities, we can think of groups of parents and educators who share their experiences of having a child with Down syndrome, or defenders of the rights of deaf people not to defer to aids and implants but instead to share the richness of silent communication via sign language. Examples can be multiplied almost *ad libitum*.

The same counts for the omnipresence of 'perfect' bodies. This is indeed very much a product of contemporary media and popular culture. Beautiful and preferably youthful bodies showing some nudity are literally everywhere, starting with posters and advertisements when one enters the airport of a new country (its absence strikes Western visitors as odd). Fat-shaming seems all around in the Western world. The warning on the mirror of a lavatory has indeed captured it rightly and pointedly.

But what about classical culture and its emphasis on harmony, symmetry, and the canon as 'a proper disposition of the flesh in the human body' (Galen, *De Plenitudine* 10), both in sculpture and medical writing? In fact, Galen's treatises such as *On the Use of the Parts* abound with remarks about the almost divine perfection of the different functions of the human body, including observations on the necessity that divine bodies were deemed to be perfect too (see, for example, the long digression on perfection and harmony in Gal. *De Usu Partium* 3.10–16 or the whole of the shorter book *De Usu Partium* 17).

But should we consider these as cases of 'ableism', insisting that a particular kind of body is preferable to another and thus 'better'? Frankly, I believe people in the ancient world had other sorrows. In a world in which life was much more fragile, the great majority of bodies seen and encountered in daily life would in no way resemble the ideal as reflected in art. Also, a considerable portion of statuettes and artefacts depicted bodies that were not perfect at all (Figure 16). For sure, there sometimes was an element of despise and mockery in these ('we' the viewers are not like 'them'), but it also showed the sheer variety that existed in human life. A recent comprehensive study suggests that such statuettes carried a positive meaning: a purgative and liberating laughter when spectators realised how the classical canon was violated. I honestly do not see how the ancient Greeks and Romans could be directly blamed for an overemphasis on bodily perfection. For sure, the classical ideal of the perfect body has not only been admired throughout the centuries, it has also been abused at the cost of those 'forgotten others' who did not or could not conform to the ideal. Nazi doctors and eugenicists are but one truly horrific example. This relates to the history of ideas and to the way such ideas were put into gruesome practice: a deliberate choice and a perverse application for which those who made such decisions are to be held fully responsible. But of course this does not justify putting the blame on classical culture for cherishing an ideal of beauty and perfection – an ideal that exists in most cultures all over the world, with both similarities and, indeed, a good deal of cultural and social packaging After all, it is possible to write a history of beauty and ugliness without recurring time and again to cultural and societal biases.

Figure 16 Grotesque bodies. Terracotta, Lamia, Thessaly, *c*.325–300 BCE. Grotesque dwarf woman holding a young girl. Sometimes interpreted as a caricature of Demeter holding young Persephone. https://commons.wikimedia .org/wiki/File:Grotesque_dwarf_Louvre_CA85.jpg

In myths and religion, Greeks and Romans dealt with infirmity and imperfection in much the same way as they did on a daily basis. With resignation, they accepted it as a fact of life. They mention it, sometimes mock or ridicule it, express fear or pity, and try to make sense out of it in one way or another. More often than not, the thing just went by unnoticed. This is not to say that suffering as such and the responsibility of the gods was never questioned in the pagan approach. Already in the *Iliad* we read of nagging doubts about whom or what is to be held responsible for the death of Zeus' Trojan son Sarpedon. It was Sarpedon's destiny to be killed by the Greek Patroclus. To Hera, Zeus expresses his doubts as to whether he should intervene and thus break what Fate had destined. Zeus only refrains from doing so since giving in on this would mean that all gods would ask for their sons to be saved. Yet 'he wept tears of blood' because of this decision (Hom. *Iliad* 16.433–8 and 459–60).

A more existential approach towards disability and healing inevitably came through with the evolution towards almighty gods and monotheism. In the ancient world, such was eminently the case in Christian thought, with the establishment of 'canonical' categories of individuals who might hope for healing according to the miracles of Jesus; with the nagging question of the theodicy and divine justice; and with a detailed mythology of gruesome punishment in hell, which would eventually find its outlet in a monument of Western European literature, Dante's *Divine Comedy*. Even here, one should be careful about a simplistic and causal approach, though. Dante is not directly to blame for the negative image of bodies considered infirm, ugly, or effeminate in later times, just as Graeco-Roman myths about, say, lame Hephaestus were not direct forerunners of the dislike of manual work performed by blacksmiths.

Why Study Ancient Myths in the Context of Disability?

I have argued that Greek and Roman myths cannot directly be used to make a case for integration of disabled people in ancient societies. On the other hand, I have also refuted a too negative approach which puts blame on these myths for cherishing persistent clichés and prejudices. In doing so, I have basically taken the standpoint of an historian of antiquity who tries to situate his sources as much as possible within the context of the world in which they were produced.

To this, a quite natural reaction would be to ask whether it makes any sense at all to study Greek and Roman mythology within a contemporary framework such as disability studies. Should an Element on the topic be written anyway? Apart from the potential for comparative research – a possibility I regularly hinted at in this Element – I would like to point to what has aptly been called the 'transhistorical power' of the Greek and Roman myths. 'Myth's malleability is

an essential part of its appeal and power,' stated Helen Morales in concluding a chapter on the use of classical myths in spirituality and New Age (2007:
114). Myths show an unusual susceptibility to various interpretations, ran-
ging from the literal to the allegorical – a too sharp distinction not being
preferable, as I argued earlier in this Element. The representation of Plutus,
the blindness of Oedipus, or the lameness of Hephaestus are three examples
of myths that were susceptible to allegorising interpretations by the ancient
authors themselves. Throughout the centuries and up to the present day,
ancient myths have shaped artworks of all sorts and inspiration. The illustrations in this Element give a glimpse of this, but the subject by itself would
be worth at least one other volume. The ancient myths show ideological
complexities that make their audience consider and reconsider time and
again. In fact, worries such as the potential impact of ableist mythological
thinking are not new at all. Worrying about myths and their content has been
part of the tradition from antiquity on. The 'tragic' guilt of Oedipus and his
consequent act of self-blinding and the 'mad' behaviour of Ajax and his
responsibility for it are examples that come readily to mind. At certain
moments, these myths even represent a sort of utopian bent, a clash of the
real with the ideal world. They transcend, as it were, the individual story.
Here, one can think of the positive collaboration between three disabled
beings expressed in the story about Orion, Cedalion, and Hephaestus.
Finally, they have the potential for prefiguration and foreshadowing, of
a world or society that maybe could exist only in the imagination. The
dream of rejuvenation, the golden and silver ages of the world, divine
recompensation in the form of soothsaying for the suffering of blindness
are some examples that appear in this Element.

   After all, it does indeed make sense to study disabilities in Greek and Roman
myths. I believe there is no need to restrict the justification of such a study by
making a political case for present-day rights and emancipation. The sheer
richness and potential of the material available should be enough by itself –
a heritage of common wealth that always brings up new interpretations, including the emancipatory one. I hope this Element has at least given a taste for
further exploration. After all, to borrow from Mary Beard, classical mythology
is a verb much more than a noun. And with Helen Morales, I express the hope
that through this Element all readers – whoever they are and from whatever
background they approach it – may find something in it 'to live their myth', just
as uncountable generations before them have done and as many no doubt will
continue to do.

Further Reading

It would be a Herculean labour and at the same time a preposterous idea to refer extensively or comprehensively to all ancient sources that mention the huge number of sometimes very divergent versions of ancient myths and legends. Such a task has been carried out at least from the last decades of the nineteenth century on, in the tradition of great encyclopaedias such as *Ausführliche Lexikon der griechischen und römischen Mythologie* (1884–1937), *Dictionnaire des Antiquités grecques et romaines* (DAGR) (1877–1919), Pauly's *Realencyclopädie der classischen Altertumswissenschaft* (RE) (1890–1980), and *Reallexikon für Antike und Christentum* (RLAC) (1933–present), all monumental testimonies to thorough classical scholarship. More concise, but more up to date for the bibliography, is *Der Neue Pauly* (DNP) (1996–2010).

The Internet provides plenty of information too. Following on major book projects such as the *Lexicon Iconographicum Mythologiae Classicae* (LIMC) (1981–99 and 2009) and the *Thesaurus Cultus et Rituum Antiquorum* (ThesCRA) (2004–14), there now is a wealth of information on WebLIMC (https://weblimc .org). This data set is regularly updated and enhanced with new documentation. A good collection, ready at hand on the Internet, with lots of references to ancient texts as well as a rich quantity of images, is the Theoi Greek Mythology Project (www.theoi.com). I recommend this source for any quick consultation.

1 Setting the Scene: Disabilities, Myths, and Religion

It would again be preposterous even to attempt to offer a list of good readings for Greek and Roman religion and mythology. I list the works I have found useful and inspirational in writing this section. Starting from these references, readers will immediately be able to find a full range of additional sources in what has become an almost limitless field. For the specific field of mythology, excellent and well-illustrated introductions are Buxton (2004) and Wiseman (2004), while I have found Morales (2007) truly inspirational in writing 'my' elementary introduction. Ogden (1997) is a classic on the tradition of crooked kings and divine punishment.

For matters such as personal belief and the possible impact of religion and myths on people's lives, the essays by Veyne (1983, 1985) remain thought-provoking and essential, though not always an easy read (see also Vegetti [1993] for the Greek world). For 'lived religion' and new tendencies in research of ex-votos, the article by Hughes (2017) is an essential introduction. See also the edited volume by Draycott and Graham (2017). On the vexed question of ancient atheism or religious scepticism, see the accessible account by Whitmarsh (2015).

The collection of essays in Buxton (1999) is a must-read for a more nuanced understanding of the presumed transition from myth to reason.

A catalogue of suicides with heroes and heroines appears in van Hooff (1990), while Friedrich (1956) has brought together an extensive number of cases of wounding in battle in the *Iliad*.

Few studies have set disabilities of gods and heroes in a comparative context. For this, Cusack (2014) is a cursory introduction while Dumézil (1948) remains a classic from a leading and most prolific scholar in the field of comparative Indo-European studies.

For definitions of disability, the inadequacy of the term, and the need for a 'practical' solution, I have drawn on my earlier work: Laes, Goodey, Rose (2013); Laes (2017, 2018, 2020). A different option, with a much wider approach to bodily imperfection, is taken by Husquin (2020). For disabilities in modern nation states, Rose (2017) is a must-read.

2 Disabled Gods and Heroes 'from Head to Toe'

Very few works specifically study disabilities in Greek and Roman mythology. Garland (2017) comes closest to my approach. Schumann (2025) became available to me when I was in the middle of the preparation of this Element. It has in-depth discussions on Thersites, Teiresias, Oedipus, Hephaestus, Philoctetes, and Plutos, and will no doubt become a standard work of reference for the matter. For more than one case, thorough articles in the elder encyclopaedias have also proven to be much worth the effort of consulting. My debts to these older pieces of scholarship are acknowledged in the bibliographical list.

For the divisions of madness and tragic madness, I have drawn on Ustinova (2018) and on the subtle analysis by Singer (2018). Thumiger (2017) is a classic on mental health and in practice deals with much more than ancient medicine. The section on war trauma and therapy is based on reported experiments in the United States (Meineck [2012]) and in the Netherlands (Tiemersma [2023]). *Achilles in Vietnam* is the title of the study by Shay (1995). Dodds (1951) is a classic on Greeks and the irrational.

For blind gods and heroes, the older studies by Esser (1961) and Lesky (1954) are still most useful. Draycott (2018) combines the study of visual impairment with the imagery of the Cyclops.

For deafness and speech impairment, almost absent in myth, I refer to Laes (2011) and (2013), as well as to Rom (2024), next to the entries by Brashear (1994), Prendesci (1999), and Tabeling (1932).

For Hephaestus, two contributions by Hall (2018) and (2021) have proved particularly insightful while the richness of the account by Schumann (2025) is unsurpassed, especially as regards the allegorical interpretations. Schmidt (1983–4) is particularly good for the sociocultural aspect of disability history and Hephaestus. The quote about the paralympics is in Lane Fox (2020). For a history of left-handedness in antiquity (and consequently also the meaning of the right hand), there is the excellent book by Wirth (2010), while Beagon (2002) is a classic on the Sergius Silus case. For the ambiguity of war wounds, see Samama (2013) and Laes (2010) with Draycott (2023) on Sergius Silus as a case for disability history and the larger history of prostheses in antiquity.

3 Other 'Oddities': Monsters, Twins, Dwarfs, and Old Age

Literature on monstrosity and monsters is again vast. For a good general introduction, see Atherton (2000) or the rich volume by Mayor (2022). For the Athenian vase representations, I drew on Hölscher (2019) while Lowe (2015) is important for concepts of the monstrous in Augustan poetry. Wasser (1909) and Voigt (1938) are unsurpassed in details on Fama-Pheme. The most thorough study on monsters and 'extraordinary' creatures, with comparative approaches and due attention to the Christian reception of the phenomenon, is Speyer (2012). For monsters and prodigies, see Beagon (2005), Cuny-le Callet (2005), and Engels (2007). On classification as well as possible identification, see Gevaert and Laes (2013) – a chapter that also elaborates on the elites' belief in the existence of monstrous creatures. For both dwarfs and twins, the studies by Dasen (1993), (2005), and (2008) are essential – all instances cited in this section stem from them. Dumézil (1994) is useful for the broad comparative approach to twins in different religions. For the specific disability interpretation of Bes, see also Kellenberger (2023). On folklore, ideology, and beliefs, Lloyd (1983) is a classic. Parkin (2003) offers interesting insights for old age in religion and mythology while the marginality of old age is explained in Wiedemann (1989).

4 Purity and Wholesomeness for Priests and Cultic Servants?

For this section, I have largely drawn on Laes (2024), which in its turn leans on excellent work by Baroin (2011), Gherchanoc (2016), Kellenberger (2019), and Wilgaux (2018). Weckwerth (2022) is illuminating for late antiquity and the role played by Judaic concepts of purity. Hall Manolaraki (2018), together with the work by Beagon (2005) (mentioned in Section 3), was essential for the observations on Pliny the Elder.

5 The Role of Christianity and Monotheism

For parts of this section, I have drawn on Laes (2024). Van Nuffelen (2010) offers a subtle analysis of Varro's criticism of traditional religion and the way

Augustine represented it. An edited volume by Mitchell and Van Nuffelen (2010) gives an excellent overview of monotheism and the pagan world. Speyer (2012) (see Section 3) offers a rich account of pagan and Christian criticism of hybrid creatures, while Funke (1981) is indispensable as an overview on pagan and Christian views of statues and images of gods. On the 'suffering' God of the Old Testament, see Schipper (2011) while Henning (2021) and Moss (2019) have done substantial work on the role of (dis)ability in the Christian discourse of eschatology and hell. Laes (2021) expands on the novelty of Christian approaches towards disability and healing. For the link between healing and (personal) sin, see Kelley (2009).

Conclusion: Disability As Anachronism or Analogy?

The reference to Indian mythology can be tracked down via https://wecapable .com/disability-indian-mythology. A much more sober approach to disabilities in India, with appropriate references and endnotes, is Miles (2017). Dumézil (1956) is a classic comparative approach to Graeco-Roman and Indian mythology while Woodard (2006) updated Dumézil's approach by paying attention to cults.

The community concept is the red thread through Rose (2003) (see Section 1). Foucault (1961) is a classic on medicalisation. Coming to terms with disability in myth and giving sense to it is implied in the title of Schumann (2025) (see Section 2), a substantial piece of work. In the paragraphs on ableism and blaming classical culture for it, I have followed, sometimes almost verbatim, Laes (2022). See also Ecco (2004) and (2007) for histories of beauty and ugliness in art and Laes (2016) on obesity and fat-shaming.

Thoughts on the purgative laughter and the positive meaning of statuettes are taken from Meintani (2022). See also Vout (2022) for engaging new work on 'imperfect' Greek and Roman bodies, as they truly were.

For the final remarks on the transhistorical power and complexities of ancient myths, I owe a great debt to the excellent and thought-provoking essay by Hall (2021) (see Section 2), as well as the charming conclusion by Morales (2007) (see Section 1).

References

Atherton, C. (2000) *Monsters and Monstrosity in Greek and Roman Culture.* Bari.

Aust, E. (1894) art. Angerona, in *RE* I, 2: *c.*2189–90.

Aust, E. (1897) art. Caeculus, in *RE* III, 1: *c.*1244–5.

Baroin, C. (2011) 'Le corps du prêtre romain dans le culte public: Début d'une enquête', in L. Bodiou, V. Mehl, and M. Soria (eds.), *Corps outragés, corps ravagés de l'Antiquité aux temps modernes.* Turnhout: 291–316.

Beagon, M. (2002) 'Beyond Comparison: M. Sergius, Fortunae Victor', in G. Clark and T. Rajak (eds.), *Philosophy and Power in the Graeco-Roman World.* Oxford: 111–32.

Beagon, M. (2005) *The Elderly Pliny on the Human Animal: Natural History Book 7. Translation with Introduction and Historical Commentary.* Oxford.

Beard, M., North, J., and Price, S. (1998) *Religions of Rome.* 2 vols. Cambridge.

Brashear, W. (1994) art. Horos, in *RLAC* XVI: *c.*574–97.

Burckhardt, A. (1928) art. Mania, in *RE* XIV, 1: *c.*1107–10.

Buxton, R. (ed.) (1999) *From Myth to Reason? Studies in the Development of Greek Thought.* Oxford.

Buxton, R. (2004) *The Complete World of Greek Mythology.* London.

Cuny-Le Callet, B. (2005) *Rome et ses monstres: 1, Naissance d'un concept philosophique et rhétorique.* Grenoble.

Cusack, C. M. (2014) 'Medicine and Mythology: Health and Healing in Indo-European Myths'. *Mentalities/Mentalités* 26, 1: 1–11.

Dasen, V. (1993) *Dwarfs in Ancient Egypt and Greece.* Oxford.

Dasen, V. (2005) *Jumeaux, jumelles dans l'Antiquité grecque et romaine.* Zurich.

Dasen, V. (2008) 'All Children Are Dwarfs': Medical Discourse and Iconography of Children's Bodies'. *Oxford Journal of Archaeology* 27, 1: 49–62.

Dodds, E. R. (1951) *The Greeks and the Irrational.* Berkeley, CA.

Dowden, K. (1992) *Religion and the Romans.* Bristol.

Dowden, K., and Livingstone, N. (2011) *A Companion to Greek Mythology.* Hoboken, NJ.

Draycott, J. (2018) 'Life As a Cyclops: Mythology and the Mockery of the Visually Impaired'. *Illinois Classical Studies* 43, 2: 404–19.

Draycott, J. (2023) *Prosthetics and Assistive Technology in Ancient Greece and Rome.* Cambridge.

Draycott, J., and Graham, E. J. (eds.) (2018) *Bodies of Evidence: Ancient Anatomical Votives Past, Present and Future.* London.

Dumézil, G. (1948) *Mitra-Varuna: Essai sur deux représentations indo-européennes de la souveraineté*. Paris. (See now Dumézil, G. [2023], *Mitra-Varuna: An Essay on Two Indo-European Representations of Sovereignty*. Translated by D. Coltman, a Critical Edition with New Introduction by S. Elden, Chicago, IL.)

Dumézil, G. (1956) *Déesses latines et mythes védiques*. Brussels.

Dumézil, G. (1994) *Le roman des jumeaux, esquisses de mythologie*. Paris.

Ecco, U. (2004) *Storia della bellezza*. Milan.

Ecco, U. (2007) *Storia della bruttezza*. Milan.

Engels, D. (2007) *Das römische Vorzeichenwesen (753–27 v.Chr.): Quellen, Terminologie, Kommentar, historische Entwicklung*. Stuttgart.

Esser, A. (1961²) *Das Antlitz der Blindheit in der Antike*. Leyden.

Fiehn, K. (1938) art. Philoktetes, in *RE* XIX, 2: *c.*2500–9.

Foucault, M. (1961) *Folie et déraison: Histoire de la folie à l'âge classique*. Paris.

Friedrich, W. H. (1956) *Verwundung und Tod in der Ilias: Homerische Darstellungsweisen*. Goettingen.

Funke, H. (1981) art. Götterbild, in *RLAC* XI (1981) *c.*659–828.

Garland, R. (1994) *Religion and the Greeks*. Bristol.

Garland, R. (2017) 'Disabilities in Tragedy and Comedy', in C. Laes (ed.), *Disability in Antiquity*. London: 154–66.

Gevaert, B., and Laes, C. (2013) 'What's in a Monster? Pliny the Elder, Teratology and Bodily Disability', in C. Laes, C. Goodey, and M. L. Rose (eds.), *Disabilities in Roman Antiquity: Disparate Bodies A Capite ad Calcem*. Leyden: 211–30.

Gherchanoc, F. (2016) *Concours de beauté et beautés du corps en Grèce ancienne: Discours et pratiques*. Bordeaux.

Hall, E. (2018) 'Hephaestus the Hobbling Humorist: The Club-Footed God in the History of Early Greek Comedy'. *Illinois Classical Studies* 43, 2: 366–87.

Hall, E. (2021) 'The Immortal Forgotten Other Gang: Dwarf Cedalion, Lame Hephaestus, and Blind Orion', in E. Adams (ed.), *Disability Studies and the Classical Body: The Forgotten Other*. London: 215–36.

Hall Manolaraki, E. (2018) 'Senses and the Sacred in Pliny's *Natural History*'. *Illinois Classical Studies* 43, 1: 207–33.

Henning, M. (2021) *Hell Hath No Fury: Gender, Disability, and the Invention of Damned Bodies in Early Christian Literature*. New Haven, CT.

Hölscher, T. (2019) *Mythenbilder und Mentalität in Athen von Kleisthenes zu den Persenkriegen: Ein Versuch zur historischen Psychologie der Griechen*. Wiesbaden.

Hughes, J. (2017) 'Souvenirs of the Self: Personal Belongings As Votive Offering in Ancient Religion'. *Religion in the Roman Empire* 3, 2: 143–63.

Husquin, C. (2020) *L'integrité du corps en question: Perceptions et représentations de l'atteinte physique dans la Rome antique.* Rennes.

Kellenberger, E. (2019) 'Muss ein Priester perfekt sein? Anförderungen an Körper, Moral und Geist der Priester in der Antike'. *Theologische Zeitschrift* 75, 2: 129–43.

Kellenberger, E. (2023) 'The Quest for Down Syndrome (and Other Symptoms) in Antiquity', in C. Laes and I. Metzler (eds.), *'Madness' in the Ancient World: Innate or Acquired? From Theoretical Concepts to Daily Life.* Turnhout: 101–22.

Kelley, N. (2009) 'The Deformed Child in Ancient Christianity', in C. B. Horn and R. P. Phenix (eds.), *Children in Late Ancient Christianity.* Tubingen: 199–216.

Laes. C. (2010) 'How Does One Do the History of Disability in Antiquity? One Thousand Years of Case Studies'. *Medicina nei Secoli* 23, 3: 915–46.

Laes, C. (2011) 'Silent Witnesses: Deaf-Mutes in Greco-Roman Antiquity'. *Classical World* 104, 4: 451–73.

Laes, C. (2013) 'Silent History? Speech Impairment in Roman Antiquity', in C. Laes, C. Goodey, and M. L. Rose (eds.), *Disabilities in Roman Antiquity: Disparate Bodies A Capite ad Calcem.* Leyden: 145–80.

Laes, C. (2016) 'Writing the Socio-cultural History of Fatness and Thinness in Graeco-Roman Antiquity'. *Medicina nei Secoli* 28, 2: 583–660.

Laes, C. (ed.) (2017) *Disability in Antiquity.* London.

Laes, C. (2018) *Disabilities and the Disabled in the Roman World: A Social and Cultural History.* Cambridge.

Laes, C. (ed.) (2020) *A Cultural History of Disability in Antiquity.* London.

Laes, C. (2021) 'How Does Graeco-Roman Antiquity Fit in the Long History of the Body and Disabilities in the Western World?' in A. Mouton (ed.), *Flesh and Bones: The Individual and His Body in the Ancient Mediterranean Basin.* Turnhout: 223–9.

Laes, C. (2022) 'All in Perfect Harmony?' *Science Museum Blog* [https://blog.sciencemuseum.org.uk/all-in-perfect-harmony].

Laes, C. (Forthcoming 2024) 'Disability and Religion', in E. Begemann, J. Bremmer, G. Petridou, and J. Rüpke (eds.), *Religion in Context.* Leyden.

Laes, C., Goodey, C. F., and Rose, M. L. (eds.) (2013) *Disabilities in Roman Antiquity: Disparate Bodies A Capite ad Calcem.* Leyden.

Lane Fox, R. (2020) *The Invention of Medicine: A History from Homer to Hippocrates.* New York.

Lesky, E. (1954) art. Blindheit, in *RLAC* II: c.433–46.

Lloyd, G. E. F. (1983) *Science, Folklore and Ideology.* Cambridge.

Lowe, D. (2015) *Monsters and Monstrosity in Augustan Poetry*. Ann Arbor, MI.

Malten, L. (1913) art. Hephaistos, in *RE* VIII, 1: *c*.311–66.

Mayor, A. (2022) *Flying Snakes and Griffin Claws and Other Classical Myths, Historical Oddities, and Scientific Curiosities*. Princeton, NJ.

Meineck, P. (2012) 'Combat Trauma and the Tragic Stage: "Restoration" by Cultural Catharsis'. *Intertexts* 16, 1: 7–24.

Meintani, A. (2022) *The Grotesque Body in Graeco-Roman Antiquity*. Berlin.

Miles, M. (2017) 'India: Demystifying Disability in Antiquity', in C. Laes (ed.), *Disability in Antiquity*. London: 90–105.

Mitchell, S., and Van Nuffelen, P. (eds.) (2010) *Monotheism between Pagans and Christians in Late Antiquity*. Leuven.

Morales, H. (2007) *Classical Mythology: A Very Short Introduction*. Oxford.

Moss, C. (2019) *Divine Bodies: Resurrecting Perfection in the New Testament and Early Christianity*. New Haven, CT.

Münzer, F. (1933) art. Mucius 10, in *RE* XVI, 1: *c*.416–23.

Ogden, D. (1997) *The Crooked Kings of Ancient Greece*. London.

Ogden, D. (2007) *A Companion to Greek Religion*. Hoboken, NJ.

Parkin, T. (2003) *Old Age in the Roman World: A Cultural and Social History*. Baltimore, MD.

Prendesci, F. (1999) art. Larunda, Mater Larum, in *DNP* 6 (1999) *c*.1156.

Rom, A. (ed.) (2024) *Other Bodies: Disability and Bodily Impairment in Early China*. London.

Rose, M. L. (2003) *The Staff of Oedipus: Transforming Disability in Ancient Greece*. Ann Arbor, MI.

Rose, S. F. (2017) *No Right to Be Idle: The Invention of Disability, 1840s–1930s*. Chapel Hill, NC.

Rüpke, J. (2001) *Die Religion der Römer*. Munich.

Rüpke, J. (ed.) (2011) *A Companion to Roman Religion*. Hoboken, NJ.

Saglio, E. (1877) art. baculum, in *DAGR* 1: 639–42.

Samama, E. (2013) 'A King Walking with Pain? On the Textual and Iconographical Images of Philip II and Other Wounded Kings', in C. Laes, C. Goodey, and M. L. Rose (eds.), *Disabilities in Roman Antiquity: Disparate Bodies A Capite ad Calcem*. Leyden: 231–48.

Schipper, J. (2011) *Disability and Isaiah's Suffering Servant*. Oxford.

Schmidt, J. (1928) art. Lyssa, in *RE* XIV, 1: *c*.69–71.

Schmidt, J. (1937) art. Oistros, in *RE* XVII, 2: *c*.2286–7.

Schmidt, M. (1983–4) 'Hephaistos lebt: Untersuchungen zur Frage der Behandlung behinderter Kinder in der Antike'. *Hephaistos* 5–6: 133–61.

Schumann, F. (Forthcoming 2025) *Der Behinderung einen Sinn verleihen: Über die Interpretation von Seh- und Gehbehinderungen bei Figuren des antiken Mythos.* Berlin.

Schwenn, F. (1934) art. Teiresias, in *RE* V, A1: *c.*129–32.

Shay, J. (1995) *Achilles in Vietnam: Combat Trauma and the Undoing of Character.* New York.

Singer, P. N. (2018) 'The Mockery of Madness: Laughter at and with Insanity in Attic Tragedy and Old Comedy'. *Illinois Classical Studies* 43, 2: 298–325.

Speyer, W. (2012) art. Mischwesen, in *RLAC* XXIV: *c.*864–926.

Tabeling, E. (1932) art. Tacita, in *RE* IV, A2: *c.*1997–8.

Thumiger, C. (2017) *A History of the Mind and Mental Health in Classical Greek Medical Thought.* Cambridge.

Tiemersma, N. (2023), 'Trauma is van alle tijden: De helende werking van de Griekse tragedie'. *Hermeneus* 95, 1: 10–17.

Totaro, P. (2016) 'La Richezza in "persona" nel "Pluto" di Aristofane'. *Lexis* 34: 144–58.

Ustinova, Y. (2018) *Divine Mania: Alteration of Consciousness in Ancient Greece.* London.

Van Hooff, A. (1990) *From Autothanasia to Suicide: Self-Killing in Classical Antiquity.* London.

Van Nuffelen, P. (2010) 'Varro's Divine Antiquities: Roman Religion As an Image of Truth'. *Classical Philology* 105, 2: 162–88.

Vegetti, M. (1993) 'L'homme et les dieux', in J.-P. Vernant (ed.), *L'homme grec.* Paris: 319–55.

Vernant, J.-P. (1990) *Mythe et réligion en Grèce ancienne.* Paris.

Versnel, H. (1996) art. Angerona, in *DNP* I (1991) *c.*761.

Veyne, P. (1983) *Les Grecs ont-ils cru à leur mythes?* Paris.

Veyne, P. (1985) 'L'Empire romain', in P. Veyne (ed.), *Histoire de la vie privée: De l'Empire romain à l'an mil.* Paris: 13–223.

Voigt, F. A. (1938) art. Pheme, in *RE* XIX, 2: *c.*1954–5.

Vout, C. (2022) *Exposed: The Greek and Roman Body.* London.

Wasser, O. (1909) art. Fama, in *RE* VI, 2: 1977–9.

Wasser, O. (1910) art. Furor, in *RE* VII, 1: *c.*382.

Weckwerth, A. (2022) *Casta placent superis: Konzeptionen kultischer Reinheit in der Spätantike.* Munster.

Whitmarsh, T. (2015) *Battling the Gods: Atheism in the Ancient World.* New York.

Wiedemann, T. (1989) *Adults and Children in the Roman Empire.* London.

Wilgaux, J. (2018) 'Infirmités et prêtrise en Méditerranée antique'. *Pallas* 106: 275–87.

Wirth, H. (2010) *Die linke Hand. Wahrnehmung und Bewertung in der griechischen und römischen Antike*. Stuttgart.

Wiseman, T. P. (2004) *The Myths of Rome*. Exeter.

Woodard, R. (2006) *Indo-European Sacred Space: Vedic and Roman Cult*. Champaign, IL.

Woodard, R. (ed.) (2006) *The Cambridge Companion to Greek Mythology*. Cambridge.

Zwicker, J. (1951) art. Plutos, in *RE* XXI, 1: *c*.1027–51.

Acknowledgements

Writing up this Element was greatly facilitated by a wonderful research stay as a Professorial Fellow at the Bonn Centre for Dependency and Slavery Studies at the University of Bonn. It is a pleasure to acknowledge my utmost thanks to both the colleagues of this Centre and to the friends and acquaintances of the Ancient History and the Classical Philology section of the same university. Many thanks also go to the Classics, Ancient History, Archaeology and Egyptology Department of the University of Manchester for granting me this research stay.

Cambridge Elements ☰

Greek and Roman Mythology

Roger D. Woodard
University of Buffalo

Roger D. Woodard is the Andrew van Vranken Raymond Professor of the Classics at the University of Buffalo (The State University of New York), formerly serving on the faculties of Swarthmore College, Johns Hopkins University, and the University of Southern California. He has held fellowships and visiting appointments at, among other institutions, the Center for Hellenic Studies of Harvard University, the American Academy in Rome, the University of Oxford. He is author or editor of numerous books, including; *Aeolic and Aeolians* (2024, CUP), *Divination and Prophecy in the Ancient Greek World* (2023, CUP); *The Textualization of the Greek Alphabet* (2014, CUP); *Myth, Ritual, and the Warrior in Roman and Indo-European Antiquity* (2013, CUP); *The Cambridge Companion to Greek Mythology* (2007, CUP).

About the Series

Cambridge Elements in Greek and Roman Mythology is a series for scholars, graduate students, and advanced undergraduates. Individual *Elements* tackle topics that are significantly more complex and multifaceted than could be accommodated in a journal or edited volume, but they will not duplicate the handbooks/companions and other conventional resources. Rather, the *Elements* format will provide an opportunity for authors to explore interesting themes and newer ideas and approaches in Greek and Roman myth. Each *Element* will present an innovative framework or interpretative strategy with sufficiently broad implications to be adapted and further developed by readers in their own work. Some *Elements* take a specific theme or question and explore it across a number of mythic traditions. Others take a detailed look at a single mythic notion or figure by way of a 'case study' in a certain interpretative approach. Yet others are devoted to the interpretative history of the discipline.

Cambridge Elements ☰

Greek and Roman Mythology

Elements in the Series

Disability and Healing in Greek and Roman Myth
Christian Laes

Printed in the United States
by Baker & Taylor Publisher Services